NORTHERN
Portugal

Travel Guide 2024

MARY ROMERO

MARY ROMERO

SCAN THE QR CODE WITH YOUR DEVICE TO GAIN ACCESS TO MORE OF MY BOOKS

Northern Portugal Travel Guide 2024

A Comprehensive Handbook Through Iconic Destinations, Rich Culture, and Hidden Charms, Complete with Detailed Maps to Enhance Your Exploration

MARY ROMERO

MAP OF NORTHERN PORTUGAL

SCAN THE QR CODE BELOW TO ACCESS FULL NORTHERN PORTUGAL MAP

CONTENTS

DEDICATION

To all the courageous spirits yearning to discover the beauty and wealth of Northern Portugal,

This book is dedicated to you, the explorers, wanderers, and seekers of new adventures. May the pages here serve as a reliable companion while you travel across Northern Portugal's breathtaking landscapes, colorful cultures, and hidden treasures.

Here's to making memories, sharing tales, and cherishing experiences that will last a lifetime. May this book encourage you to discover every nook, embrace every culture, and cherish every second of your journey through this fascinating region.

With deepest thanks for choosing to explore with us,

MARY ROMERO

PURPOSE OF THE BOOK

Dear Readers,

This book is intended to be your ultimate companion and guide as you discover the marvels of Northern Portugal in 2024. Our goal is to give you thorough insights, practical advice, and insider information to help you enjoy every element of your trip through this interesting region.

Whether you're interested in the renowned sites, the rich cultural history, the beautiful seaside villages, or the magnificent scenery, this book will meet your every desire. From comprehensive itineraries and must-see sights to hidden treasures off the main track, we've compiled a wealth of information to help you make the most of your stay in Northern Portugal. More than just a travel guide, this book opens the door to extraordinary experiences, significant friendships, and lifetime memories. We hope it encourages you to thoroughly immerse yourself in Northern Portugal's beauty and diversity, allowing you to discover its hidden gems and the genuine soul of this magnificent place.

So, whether you're an experienced traveler or going on your first voyage, we encourage you to join us on this journey of exploration, discovery, and amazement. Northern Portugal awaits; let this book be your key to unlocking its limitless potential.

Enjoy your travels!

FACTS ABOUT NORTHERN PORTUGAL

Below are some of the most fascinating facts about Northern Portugal which we found very helpful for your journey.

1. Northern Portugal is renowned for its breathtaking scenery, which includes lush green mountains, scenic valleys, and a dramatic coastline.

2. Porto, Portugal's second-largest city, is well-known for its historic core, Port wine industry, and the renowned Dom Luís I Bridge.

3. Guimarães, often known as the "birthplace of Portugal," is a UNESCO World Heritage Site in Northern Portugal.

4. Northern Portugal is home to many UNESCO World Heritage Sites, including the Historic Centre of Porto, the Alto Douro Wine Region, and the Prehistoric Rock-Art Sites of the Côa Valley and Siege Verde.

5. The Douro Valley, located in Northern Portugal, is one of the world's oldest wine areas and is well-known for producing premium Port wine.

6. Braga, often known as the "City of Archbishops," is a medieval city in Northern Portugal noted for its Catholic legacy and Baroque architecture.

7. Peneda-Gerês National Park, Portugal's sole national park, is located in northern Portugal and

has stunning landscapes, hiking paths, and rich species.

8. The Minho area in Northern Portugal is famous for its verdant scenery, quaint towns, and traditional Portuguese food.

9. The city of Viana do Castelo, in Northern Portugal, is well-known for its bright folklore events and beautiful traditional costumes.

10. Trás-os-Montes in northern Portugal is known for its rocky landscape, traditional rural culture, and hearty food.

11. Northern Portugal has a diverse cultural background, with Celtic, Roman, and Moorish influences visible in its architecture, gastronomy, and rituals.

Guimarães, the birthplace of Portugal's first monarch, Afonso Henriques, is known as the "cradle of the Portuguese nationality".

13. The Barcelos Rooster, an emblem of Portuguese culture, originates in Northern Portugal and is linked to a famous mythology.

14. Traditional folk music and dance, such as the Fado de Coimbra and the Pauliteiros de Miranda, are essential components of northern Portuguese culture.

15. The Alto Minho region is famous for its Vinho Verde wine, a light and crisp wine made from young grapes cultivated in the rich valleys of the Minho River.

16. Braga is home to the Bom Jesus do Monte Sanctuary, a well-known pilgrimage site with a magnificent Baroque stairway and breathtaking views of the surrounding area.

17. Northern Portugal has a rich marine culture, with fishing communities along the coast and ancient ports like Vila do Conde and Matosinhos.

18. The city of Vila Nova de Gaia, located over the river from Porto, has various wine cellars where tourists may sample and learn about Port wine manufacturing.

19. The ancient village of Ponte de Lima, in Northern Portugal, is known for its medieval bridge, lovely gardens, and yearly horse show.

20. Northern Portugal has a range of outdoor activities, such as hiking, surfing, and mountain biking, making it a perfect location for nature lovers and adventure seekers.

These facts offer a look into Northern Portugal's rich history, culture, and natural beauty, enticing visitors to discover its various landscapes and dynamic cities.

INTRODUCTION TO NORTHERN PORTUGAL

Overview Of The Region

Northern Portugal, an area of spectacular beauty and rich cultural legacy, entices visitors with its various landscapes, medieval cities, and quaint seaside villages. This location, located in Portugal's northwest corner, offers a plethora of activities that await discovery.

Northern Portugal has diverse terrain, including lush green valleys, rolling hills, craggy mountains, and a stunning coastline. The territory is surrounded by Spain to the east and the Atlantic Ocean to the west, creating a beautiful contrast in sceneries. The Douro River, one of Europe's main rivers, flows through the region, creating incredibly magnificent valleys and vineyards along the way. The region boasts dynamic cities and towns, each with its distinct character and attraction. Porto, Portugal's second-largest city, serves as the region's cultural and economic capital, known for its historic center, port wine production, and breathtaking riverbank vistas. Guimarães, Portugal's birthplace, has a rich history and maintained architecture. Other important attractions are Braga, which is noted for its religious significance, and Barcelos, which is famed for its vibrant pottery and culture.

Northern Portugal's architecture, culture, and food reflect its rich cultural legacy. Visitors may explore centuries-old castles, Romanesque cathedrals, and picturesque towns trapped in time. Folk music, dancing, and festivals provide glimpses into the region's complex cultural tapestry, while gastronomic pleasures such as substantial stews, fresh seafood, and pastries tempt the taste buds and highlight the region's culinary history.

Northern Portugal has several outdoor activities for those who enjoy them. There are plenty of opportunities for adventure, from hiking and riding in Portugal's sole national park, Peneda-Gerês, to surfing along Costa Verde's rough coastline. The Douro Valley, a UNESCO World Heritage Site, welcomes visitors to explore its terraced vineyards, sample world-class wines, and cruise the river in traditional Rabelo boats. Northern Portugal's economic growth has been driven by tourism, technology, and industry. The region's cities are hubs of innovation and entrepreneurship, while the rural areas remain closely tied to traditional sectors such as agriculture and handicraft. This fusion of old and contemporary produces a dynamic and ever-changing environment with something for every tourist.

Northern Portugal offers a unique blend of history, culture, and natural beauty, making for an outstanding travel experience. Northern Portugal welcomes you with open arms and promises to make a lasting effect on your heart and spirit, whether you're discovering historic cities, experiencing local cuisine, or spending time in the great outdoors.

Brief History And Cultural Significance Of Northern Portugal

Northern Portugal's story spans ancient civilizations to medieval kingdoms and beyond, weaving themes of conquest, discovery, and survival. Early human presence in Northern Portugal may be traced back to the Paleolithic era, with archaeological sites like the Côa Valley displaying archaic rock art that sheds light on our predecessors' lifestyle. Various tribes and civilizations, like the Celts and the Lusitanians, settled in the region over time, leaving remnants of their customs and traditions behind.

During the Roman invasion of the Iberian Peninsula in the first century BCE, Northern Portugal, also known as Lusitania, became a member of the Roman Empire. The Romans founded colonies, constructed highways, and introduced new agricultural techniques, transforming the environment and leaving an indelible mark on the region's culture and infrastructure. Important Roman ruins, such as the city of Braga (Bracara Augusta), continue to offer a testament to this time in history.

Medieval Kingdoms: During the early Middle Ages, Northern Portugal was a battleground for kingdoms seeking power and domination. The formation of the County of Portugal in the ninth century set the groundwork for the rise of the Portuguese nation. Guimarães, known as the "Cradle of Portugal," is historically noteworthy as the birthplace of Portugal's first monarch, Afonso I. It has been designated a UNESCO World Heritage Site for its well-preserved medieval architecture.

During the 15th and 16th centuries, Portugal experienced a golden period of discovery, with northern ports like Porto playing a vital role in marine commerce. Portuguese navigators, notably Vasco da Gama and Ferdinand Magellan sailed from these beaches in pursuit of new trade routes and territories, ushering in a period of global discovery and cultural interchange. The money returned from these excursions aided the growth of art, architecture, and commerce in Northern Portugal.

Northern Portugal's cultural significance is reflected in its architecture, traditions, and art. The region is home to many UNESCO World Past Sites, including the Historic Centre of Porto, the Douro Valley Wine Region, and the Bom Jesus do Monte Sanctuary in Braga, which showcase its architectural and religious past. Traditional events, like the São João Festival in Porto and the Romaria de São Torcato in Guimarães, highlight the region's cultural identity and foster communal spirit and tradition. Northern Portugal's history demonstrates the perseverance and ingenuity of its people, who have preserved their cultural legacy throughout centuries of upheaval. Northern Portugal's history spans ancient civilizations, medieval kingdoms, and the era of discovery, creating the region's identity and character.

What To Expect From The Guide

This thorough guide has been painstakingly created to equip you with everything you need to make the most of your trip through this fascinating region. Here's what to expect:

1. Detailed Destination Coverage: Our guide will take you on a tour of Northern Portugal's various landscapes, ancient cities, and beautiful villages. From the busy streets of Porto to the peaceful coastlines of the Douro Valley, we cover it all, ensuring that no hidden treasure is missed.

2. Insider advice and suggestions: Discover Northern Portugal's secrets with our insider advice and suggestions. If you're looking for the greatest local cuisine, off-the-beaten-path sites, or insider information on cultural events, we've got you covered.

3. Use our practical travel knowledge to easily navigate Northern Portugal. From transportation alternatives and lodging recommendations to keywords and local traditions, we provide everything you need to travel comfortably and safely.

4. Cultural Insights: Immerse yourself in Northern Portugal's rich cultural legacy with our in-depth insights. Discover the region's interesting history, customs, and festivals, and develop a better grasp of its vibrant cultural tapestry.

5. Outdoor experiences: Explore the natural splendor of Northern Portugal and go on unique outdoor experiences. Whether you're hiking in the Peneda-Gerês National Park, discovering the Douro

Valley wines, or surfing along the rough coastline, we'll lead you to the greatest outdoor adventures.

6. customizable Itineraries: Our customizable itineraries allow you to tailor your Northern Portugal experience to your own interests and preferences. Whether you have a week or a month to explore, we offer example itineraries to fit every timetable or travel style.

7. Updated Information: Stay current with the most recent information and advice for touring Northern Portugal in 2024. Our guide is regularly updated to reflect changes in attractions, services, and travel circumstances, so you always have the most up-to-date information.

This guide will help you have wonderful experiences in Northern Portugal. Whether you're a first-time visitor or an experienced traveler, we're convinced that our in-depth coverage, insider insights, and practical guidance will improve every part of your trip. Prepare to go on an unforgettable vacation as we explore the splendor of Northern Portugal.

PLANNING YOUR TRIP

Best Time To Visit Northern Portugal

Choosing the best time to visit Northern Portugal is critical for enjoying everything this fascinating area has to offer. But worry no more this complete guide outline to help you plan your trip:

1. Spring (March-May): Springtime in Northern Portugal offers blossoming flowers, pleasant weather, and fewer visitors, making it a perfect season to visit. You'll see the landscape come alive with vivid hues, especially in the Douro Valley wineries. This time of year is ideal for outdoor activities like trekking and touring ancient places.

2. Summer (June-August): The prime tourism season in Northern Portugal, with long sunny days and mild temperatures, attracts travelers from all over the world. Coastal places, such as Porto and the beaches of Costa Verde, are especially popular during this time. However, be prepared for increased crowds and higher expenses, particularly in popular tourist destinations.

3. Fall (September to November): Northern Portugal offers temperate weather, fewer people, and gorgeous autumn foliage, making it an ideal season to visit. The Douro Valley's grape harvest season provides a unique opportunity to learn about local winemaking traditions and attend festivities. Cultural activities and gastronomy festivals are also prevalent at this period.

4. Winter (December–February): Northern Portugal has colder temperatures and occasional rains, especially around the coast. While outdoor activities may be limited, this season presents an opportunity to visit the region's cultural attractions, such as museums, galleries, and historic buildings, without the crowds. The joyous mood of the Christmas season, particularly in Porto, gives a unique dimension to winter trips.

➢ Factors To Consider:

Weather: Northern Portugal has a Mediterranean climate, with moderate winters and scorching summers. However, weather patterns might differ based on location and height. Plan your vacation around local festivals and events, like São João in Porto or Festa da Senhora da Agonia in Viana do Castelo, to fully experience the region's culture.

Personal Preferences: The ideal time to visit Northern Portugal is ultimately determined by your interests and preferences. Whether you enjoy outdoor activities, cultural events, or just avoiding crowds, there is an ideal time for everyone. Northern Portugal caters to a diverse range of travelers throughout the year. There is never a bad time to visit this fascinating area (Northern Portugal), whether you're touring historic sites, sampling local food, or taking in the natural splendor. Consider the elements listed above to choose the optimal time for your Northern Portugal excursion and prepare for an amazing experience.

Entry Requirements And Visa Information Into Northern Portugal

Before departing on your journey to Northern Portugal, you should acquaint yourself with the entrance criteria and visa information to guarantee a smooth and hassle-free travel experience. Here's what you should know.

1. Passport Requirement:

All tourists to Portugal, including Northern Portugal, must have a valid passport. Ensure that your passport is valid for at least six months after your anticipated departure date from Portugal.

2. Visa requirements:

Citizens of the European Union (EU), the European Economic Area (EEA), and Switzerland do not require a visa to visit Portugal for short stays (up to 90 days) for tourist, business, or family purposes. Citizens of several other countries, including the United States, Canada, Australia, and New Zealand, can enter Portugal without a visa for short periods (up to 90 days) for tourism or business.

However, tourists from some countries may need a Schengen visa to enter Portugal. Before going, make sure you understand the precise visa requirements for your nationality. Longer stays or objectives such as job, education, or residency may need additional visa requirements. It is best to contact the nearest Portuguese embassy or consulate for complete visa information and application processes well in advance of your trip.

3. Schengen Area Regulations:

Portugal is a member of the Schengen Area, which provides for passport-free travel among participating nations. Travelers entering Portugal from another Schengen nation do not need to go through passport control, but they must have the proper travel documentation and complete the entrance conditions.

4. COVID-19 Travel Restrictions.

Due to the continuing COVID-19 epidemic, extra travel restrictions and entry procedures may be in effect. These might include pre-travel testing, quarantine upon arrival, or documentation of immunization or recovery from COVID-19.

It is critical to remain up to date on the latest travel advisories and entrance requirements from official sources, such as the Portuguese government and appropriate health agencies.

5. Additional documentation:

While not usually necessary, it is suggested to include supplementary papers such as evidence of lodging, return or onward travel plans, travel insurance, and enough money to cover your stay in Portugal. Understanding the entrance procedures and visa information for Northern Portugal is essential for a smooth travel experience. By ensuring that you have the essential documentation and satisfy all entrance conditions, you may enjoy the beauties of Northern Portugal without any hassle. Remember to remain up to date on any revisions or changes to entrance criteria, particularly given the changing global travel environment. Safe travels!

Budgeting And Cost Considerations

A journey to Northern Portugal necessitates careful budgeting and expense considerations to achieve a pleasurable and stress-free travel experience. This detailed handbook will help you efficiently manage your funds.

1. Accommodation.

Northern Portugal has a variety of lodging alternatives to suit all budgets, from luxury hotels and boutique guesthouses to low-cost hostels and rental flats. Accommodation prices vary according to location, season, and facilities. Accommodations in big cities such as Porto are often more costly than those in smaller towns or rural locations.

Consider reserving your lodgings ahead of time, especially during busy tourist seasons, to ensure the greatest pricing and availability.

2. Transportation:

Northern Portugal is quite economical to travel by rail, bus, rental vehicle, or taxi. Public transportation, such as trains and buses, is an inexpensive means to travel between cities and villages. Portugal's train system, run by CP (Comboios de Portugal), provides dependable and fairly priced connections to important locations.

Rental automobiles provide flexibility and convenience for visiting Northern Portugal's rural locations and off-the-beaten-path attractions. However, keep in mind that there will be other charges, such as gasoline, tolls, and parking fees.

Consider purchasing transportation tickets or discount cards, like the Porto Card, that provide discounts on public transportation, attractions, and activities.

3. Dining & Food Costs:

Northern Portugal is well-known for its tasty and economical food, which includes a broad range of meals to suit every taste and budget. Dining at local restaurants and cafés may be rather affordable, especially when compared to other European destinations. Look for "menu do dia" (menu of the day) alternatives, which frequently feature a set meal for a predetermined price.

Take advantage of local markets and grocery stores to buy fresh vegetables, snacks, and picnic items at reasonable costs.

Tasting Portugal's famed port wine and indulging in regional delicacies such as bacalhau (salted codfish) may provide a memorable gastronomic experience without breaking the wallet.

4. Sights and Activities:

Many of Northern Portugal's attractions, including historic monuments, museums, and natural marvels, provide free or reduced entry to specific groups, such as the elderly, students, and children.

Consider prioritizing your must-see destinations and budgeting appropriately. Look for combo tickets or city passes that provide discounts at various sites.

Take advantage of free walking tours, hiking paths, and panoramic vistas to discover Northern Portugal's splendor without spending a cent.

5. Miscellaneous expenses:

Don't forget to account for incidental expenses like souvenirs, gratuities, and unexpected fees. Setting away a small emergency fund might assist cover unforeseen bills and crises. Consider utilizing a travel budgeting tool or spreadsheet to keep track of your costs and remain on budget during your trip.

By properly planning and budgeting for your vacation to Northern Portugal, you may enjoy everything this wonderful region has to offer without going broke. Whether you're touring ancient cities, indulging in excellent cuisine, or taking in the natural beauty, keeping these financial concerns in mind can help you have a wonderful and economical trip.

Transportation Options

Northern Portugal's various landscapes and dynamic cities are easily navigated thanks to a choice of transportation alternatives that cater to any traveler's needs. Here's a detailed guide to assist you in determining the best method to travel around:

Trains:

Portugal's rail network, operated by CP (Comboios de Portugal), provides dependable and pleasant service between major cities and communities in Northern Portugal. The Alfa Pendular and Intercidades trains offer high-speed connections between Porto, Lisbon, and other locations, making it easier to travel vast distances.

Regional and urban trains connect smaller towns and villages, making them perfect for visiting Northern Portugal's landscape and coastline.

Buses:

A vast network of regional and intercity buses provides easy and economical transit across Northern Portugal. Rede Expressos and Rodonorte are two main bus companies that operate routes between the region's major cities and communities. These buses are popular among budget-conscious passengers since they have regular departures and provide nice facilities.

STCP (Sociedade de Transportes Colectivos do Porto) and other municipal corporations provide local buses that service urban areas, making it easy to visit Porto and neighboring cities.

Rental cars:

Renting a car allows you to explore Northern Portugal at your own leisure, which is especially useful if you want to visit rural areas or off-the-beaten-path places. Major car rental firms have locations in airports, rail stations, and city centers across Northern Portugal, offering a diverse range of automobiles to meet your needs.

Be wary of toll roads, parking limits, and driving prohibitions, particularly in congested metropolitan areas.

Metro and trams:

Porto has an effective metro system that provides quick and easy transportation across the city and suburbs. The metro network connects significant tourist destinations such as the old city center, port wine cellars, and beaches.

The ancient tram line (Tram 22) in Porto is a major tourist attraction, providing a magnificent ride along the Douro River coastline and through the lovely streets of the Ribeira region.

Taxis and Ridesharing:

Taxis are frequently accessible throughout Northern Portugal's major towns and tourist destinations, making them an ideal mode of transportation for short journeys or to and from airports and train stations.

Ride-sharing services like Uber and Bolt are also accessible in Porto and other cities, providing an alternative to traditional taxis with clear pricing and easy smartphone booking.

6. Cycling and walking:

Exploring Northern Portugal by bicycle or on foot is a wonderful way to appreciate the area's natural beauty and cultural legacy. Many cities and villages in Northern Portugal have bike rentals and dedicated riding paths, allowing you to explore at your own leisure while being active and environmentally responsible.

Northern Portugal's transportation alternatives are broad, making it easy, efficient, and entertaining to move about. Whether you like the flexibility of renting a vehicle, the ease of public transit, or the freedom of cycling, there is a method of transportation that will meet your needs. Plan your trip intelligently and have a memorable tour across Northern Portugal's stunning landscapes and ancient cities.

EXPLORING NORTHERN PORTUGAL: REGIONS AND CITIES

Porto And Its Surroundings

Porto, located along the banks of the Douro River, is a city rich in history, culture, and beauty. Porto, Portugal's second-largest city, serves as the northern region's economic and cultural center. Its beautiful streets, historical sites, and bustling atmosphere make it a must-see destination for visitors from all over the world. In this detailed tour, we'll explore Porto and its surroundings, revealing the hidden jewels and famous landmarks that make this place a genuine treasure.

Porto, commonly known as Oporto, has a rich maritime history spanning centuries. Its historic center, a UNESCO World Heritage Site, demonstrates its architectural and cultural value. Porto is a charming city with prominent landmarks such as the Dom Luís I Bridge and the colorful Ribeira area with small cobblestone alleyways.

Sightseeing in Porto: Start with the city's renowned sights. Begin with a walk along the Ribeira coastline, where you can see the lovely façade of historic townhouses and observe traditional Rabelo boats bobbing in the river. Visit the famed port wine cellars in Vila Nova de Gaia, accessible via the Dom Luís I Bridge. Tastings and tours are available.

Continue your sightseeing trip by seeing the Sé church, a majestic Romanesque church dating back to the 12th century. Climb the bell tower to get panoramic views of the city and the river below. Don't miss the famous Livraria Lello, a lovely bookstore known for its spectacular Art Nouveau building and link to J.K. Rowling, the author of the Harry Potter books.

For art fans, the Serralves Museum of Contemporary Art is a must-see. The museum, housed in a spectacular Art Deco structure surrounded by lush gardens, features a broad collection of modern and contemporary artworks by Portuguese and international artists.

Porto's gastronomic pleasures are a must-try for any visitor. Porto is well-known for its robust and savory food, which reflects the region's strong marine background and emphasis on fresh ingredients. Try typical Portuguese delicacies like bacalhau à brás (codfish with scrambled eggs and potatoes), francesinha (a hefty sandwich with layers of meat and cheese slathered in a spicy sauce), and caldo verde (a soothing kale soup).

Explore the city's vibrant food markets, including the Mercado do Bolhão, where you can get fresh fruit, meats, cheeses, and artisanal items. For a genuine sense of Porto, visit one of the city's historic tasks or taverns, where you can savor authentic Portuguese food in a warm and inviting setting.

Exploring Porto's Surroundings: In addition to the city's attractions, the neighboring locations are also worth exploring. Explore outside the city boundaries to find lovely villages, breathtaking landscapes, and ancient places that provide insight into Northern Portugal's rich cultural past.

One such place is the Douro Valley, which is known for its stunning vineyards, terraced slopes, and world-class wines. Take a picturesque river cruise down the Douro River, stopping at vineyards and quintas (wine estates) along the way to taste the region's famed port wines and Vinho Verde.

Guimarães, also known as the "birthplace of Portugal," is a nearby historic city. Discover the city's historic alleyways, see Guimarães Castle, and learn about the country's history in the Palace of the Dukes of Braganza.

For a taste of the sea, visit Matosinhos, a coastal town noted for its sandy beaches, delicious seafood restaurants, and bustling fishing port. Relax on the beautiful beaches of Praia de Matosinhos, watch surfers ride the waves, and have a seafood feast at one of the waterfront restaurants.

Porto and its surroundings provide a plethora of activities for those seeking history, culture, and gastronomic pleasures. From the cobblestone alleyways of the old town to the luscious vineyards of the Douro Valley, this region enchants travelers with its beauty, charm, and welcoming friendliness. Whether you're visiting Porto's ancient buildings, eating its delectable food, or heading into the countryside, you'll make memories that last a lifetime in this charming corner of Northern Portugal.

The Douro Valley

Located between Northern Portugal's undulating hills and flowing riverbanks is the Douro Valley, an area of spectacular beauty, rich history, and world-renowned wines. This UNESCO World Heritage Site, located along the Douro River, is known for its terraced vineyards, medieval Quintas (wine estates), and attractive riverfront communities. In this detailed itinerary, we'll take a journey across the Douro Valley, discovering hidden treasures and learning about its winemaking legacy.

The Douro Valley, sometimes known as the "Enchanted Valley," is among the world's oldest wine-producing regions. Its rocky topography, with steep slopes and schist soil, provides ideal conditions for growing grapes, notably the indigenous varietals used to make port wine.

The Douro Valley offers breathtaking scenery. Terraced vineyards tumble down the hillsides, following the river's bends and forming a tapestry of green and gold that extends as far as the eye can see. Olive groves, almond orchards, and fruit trees dot the terrain, contributing to the area's rural beauty.

The Douro Valley's winemaking culture revolves around old estates known as quintas. Many of these quintas invite tourists, providing guided tours, tastings, and immersive experiences that reveal the winemaking process. Quinta do Vallado is one such estate, a family-owned winery that has been in operation since 1716. Visitors at Quinta do Vallado may visit the vines, view the cellars, and taste a variety of their award-winning wines, including port and table wines. Quinta do Pacheca is another must-see Quinta, with a gorgeous position overlooking the Douro River. In addition to wine tastings and excursions, Quinta do Pacheca provides exquisite lodgings in wine barrels, giving guests a one-of-a-kind opportunity to sleep among the vineyards.

Taking a river cruise down the Douro River is a great opportunity to see the Douro Valley's splendor. These picturesque excursions provide panoramic views of the vine-covered hillsides, terraced landscapes, and lovely towns that border the river banks.

Several firms provide day cruises, multi-day cruises, and even wine-themed cruises that include sightseeing, wine tastings, and visits to nearby vineyards. Whether you travel in a traditional Rabelo boat or a contemporary river cruise ship, you'll be treated to breathtaking sights and a wonderful ride through the heart of the Douro Valley.

The Douro Valley is known for its natural beauty, winemaking heritage, and rich cultural traditions. Charming villages and towns dot the landscape, with narrow cobblestone lanes, whitewashed buildings, and terracotta rooftops that appear to stop time.

Pinhão is a hamlet known as the entryway to the Douro Valley. You may stroll along the riverbank promenade, see the old train station with azulejo tile panels portraying winemaking scenes, and wander through the picturesque alleys packed with wine shops and cafes.

For a flavor of local culture, attend one of the many festivals and events held throughout the year. From grape harvest festivities in the fall to traditional processions and religious celebrations, these events provide insight into the customs and traditions that have molded life in the Douro Valley over decades.

The Douro Valley is a breathtakingly beautiful place where the ageless rhythms of winemaking and the calm flow of the river combine to produce a really spectacular experience. Whether you're sipping port wine at a historic Quinta, boating the Douro River, or touring picturesque communities steeped in history, every moment in the Douro Valley is memorable. So come, immerse yourself in the gorgeous scenery and rich traditions of this magnificent wine area, and experience the Douro Valley's charm for yourself.

Minho Region

Placed in the lush green landscapes of Northern Portugal, the Minho Region entices visitors with its rich history, vibrant culture, and breathtaking natural beauty. From lovely old cities to scenic countryside and magnificent coastline, the Minho Region has a wide range of experiences ready to be explored. In this thorough tour, we'll look at the best of the Minho Region, including its hidden jewels and renowned sites.

Introduction to Minho Region:

The Minho Region lies in the northwest of Portugal, bordering Spain to the east and the Atlantic Ocean to the west. It is well-known for its lush vegetation, rich valleys, and mild climate, making it an ideal destination for nature lovers and outdoor enthusiasts. The region's rich cultural past can be seen in its historic cities, quaint villages, and old sites, and its friendly welcome and exquisite cuisine further add to its appeal.

Explore the Minho Region's bustling cities, each with its own unique character and attractions. Braga dubbed the "Rome of Portugal," is a city rich in religious heritage, with spectacular buildings like the Bom Jesus do Monte Sanctuary and Sé Cathedral. Explore the historic center's meandering lanes, which are studded with stunning churches, museums, and cafés.

Guimarães, known as the "birthplace of Portugal," is located just a short drive from Braga. Explore the medieval neighborhood, a UNESCO World Heritage

Site, with its cobblestone lanes, Guimarães Castle, and Palace of the Dukes of Braganza.

For a taste of coastal splendor, visit Viana do Castelo, a lovely village on the Atlantic coast. Explore the ancient center's colorful buildings and narrow alleyways, climb the hilltop Sanctuary of Santa Luzia for panoramic views of the coast, and unwind on the stunning beaches of Praia do Cabedelo and Praia Norte. Explore the Minho Region's rich cultural legacy through traditional festivals, historic buildings, and municipal museums and galleries. The region hosts several festivals and festivities, including the Festas de São João in Braga, the Romaria da Nossa Senhora da Agonia in Viana do Castelo, and the Festas Gualterianas in Guimarães.

History fans will appreciate the abundance of historic attractions in the Minho Region, which range from ancient Roman ruins to medieval castles and baroque mansions. Highlights include the Roman settlement of Citânia de Briteiros in Guimarães, the medieval Castle of Santa Maria da Feira, and the baroque Mateus Palace in Vila Real. Art lovers can find something to appreciate in the Minho Region's museums and galleries, which house a wide range of artworks spanning centuries. Don't miss the Alberto Sampaio Museum and the Biscainhos Museum in Braga, the Museum of Contemporary Art in Viana do Castelo, or the Amadeo de Souza-Cardoso Museum in Amarante.

Outdoor Adventures in the Minho Region:

The region's spectacular natural landscapes offer ideal backdrops for outdoor sports. Discover the steep highlands of the Peneda-Gerês National Park, where you can climb through ancient forests, bathe in crystal-clear lakes, and see animals like wild horses and golden eagles.

The region's rivers and beaches provide chances for water sports like kayaking, stand-up paddleboarding, and surfing. Take a leisurely boat cruise down the Lima River, or explore Esposende and Caminha beaches for some sun, sand, and sea. The Minho Region's food features fresh local products and traditional recipes passed down through generations, making it a must-try for any visitor. Try regional delicacies like caldo green (a robust kale soup), arroz de sarrabulho (a savory rice dish with a pig), and bacalhau à Braga.

Pair your dinner with a glass of vinho verde, the region's famed young wine, which has sharp acidity and a faint effervescence. Visit local markets and culinary festivals to sample specialty cheeses, sausages, and pastries. The Minho Region provides many experiences for people interested in history, culture, nature, and food. Discover the beauty and diversity of Northern Portugal by visiting ancient cities like Braga, Guimarães, and Viana do Castelo, hiking in the Peneda-Gerês National Park, and enjoying regional cuisine. Plan your trip carefully and prepare to make memories that will last a lifetime in the Minho Region.

Trás-Os-Montes

Trás-os-Montes, located in the northeastern part of Portugal, entices visitors with its rough scenery, rich cultural history, and kind friendliness. This region, which translates as "Behind the Mountains" in Portuguese, is noted for its secluded settlements, historic customs, and breathtaking natural beauty. In this detailed tour, we will explore the highlights of Trás-os-Montes, including its hidden jewels and renowned sites.

Introduction to Trás-os-Montes.

Trás-os-Montes is a land of contrasts, with towering mountains giving way to verdant valleys, flowing rivers, and rolling plains. Its secluded location and steep terrain have preserved its ancient way of life, making it an ideal destination for people seeking authenticity and tranquillity. Trás-os-Montes, with its medieval cities and villages and stunning natural landscapes, provides a look into Portugal's rich cultural and natural legacy.

Explore Trás-os-Montes' ancient cities and villages, each with unique charm and attractions. Bragança, the region's major city, with an outstanding medieval fortress that dominates the skyline. Explore the old town's small lanes, stop at the Domus Municipal, a one-of-a-kind medieval edifice with an inverted cone shape, and take in the panoramic views from the castle's towers. Travel farther into the countryside to discover picturesque communities like Miranda do Douro, which is known for its traditional architecture and cultural history. Explore the old center, which has well-preserved residences and granite structures, as well as the Cathedral of Miranda do Douro, and learn about the region's distinct cultural combination of Portuguese and Mirandese traditions.

Visit Montalegre, a lovely town with bustling festivals, to get a flavor of country life. Explore the historic castle ruins, stroll through the cobblestone alleyways of the old town, and savor local specialties like the famed smoked sausages and cured beef.

Trás-os-Montes boasts breathtaking natural settings that provide limitless chances for outdoor activities. Explore the steep slopes of Montesinho Natural Park, where you can climb through virgin woods, see species like wild boar and deer, and take in spectacular views of the surrounding landscape. The region's rivers and lakes make an ideal environment for water-based sports, including fishing, kayaking, and swimming. The Douro River, which forms Trás-os-Montes' southern boundary, provides magnificent boat tours through the gorgeous Douro Valley, which is dotted with terraced vineyards and old estates.

Cultural experiences in Trás-os-Montes:

Participate in Trás-os-Montes' rich cultural legacy by attending traditional festivals, visiting local museums and galleries, and tasting real cuisine. The region is recognized for its bright festivals and festivities, such as Mogadouro's Bull Festival, Vinhais' Chestnut Festival, and Podence's Carnival, which is famed for its Caretos masks and colorful parades.

Visit the Museum of Abade de Baçal in Bragança to learn about the region's history and cultural heritage, such as traditional crafts, folklore, and agricultural methods. Visit local artisan workshops and markets to find handcrafted pottery, textiles, and other crafts that highlight the region's creative flair and ingenuity.

Culinary delights of Trás-os-Montes:

No trip to Trás-os-Montes is complete without trying its delectable gastronomy, which represents the region's agricultural traditions and natural riches. Enjoy classic delicacies like the substantial cozido à portuguesa (Portuguese stew), the delicious posta mirandesa (grilled beef steak), and the decadent bola de carne. Pair your dinner with a glass of local wine or port made in the Douro Valley vineyards and other wine-growing districts of Trás-os-Montes. Visit local markets and fairs to sample regional delicacies like honey, cheese, olives, and chestnuts and become immersed in the smells and scents of this real and diverse gastronomic scene.

Trás-os-Montes has a plethora of opportunities for those seeking adventure, culture, and natural beauty. Whether you're visiting old villages, trekking in the mountains, or enjoying traditional food, the rough terrain and friendly hospitality of this lovely area will capture you. Plan your trip intelligently and expect to have experiences that will last a lifetime in Trás-os-Montes.

Beira Alta

Lies in the heart of Northern Portugal, Beira Alta entices visitors with its gorgeous scenery, rich cultural heritage, and welcoming hospitality. This ancient region, noted for its quaint villages, luscious vineyards, and breathtaking mountains, has a multitude of experiences just waiting to be discovered. In this detailed tour, we will explore the highlights of Beira Alta, including its hidden jewels and renowned sites.

Beira Alta, or "Upper Beira" in English, is an area of diverse terrain, including undulating hills, rich valleys, rough mountains, and rivers. Beira Alta is located in the center section of Northern Portugal, surrounded by the Douro River to the north and the Serra da Estrela mountain range to the south. Its strategic position has molded its history and culture, producing an intriguing combination of traditions and influences. Explore Beira Alta's ancient cities and towns, each with unique charm and attractions. Viseu, the region's main city, is renowned for its well-preserved old core, which has exquisite plazas, ancient churches, and lovely cobblestone lanes. Explore the Sé Cathedral, a spectacular example of Portuguese Gothic architecture, and the Grão Vasco Museum, which has an amazing collection of Renaissance art.

Travel farther into the countryside to see picturesque communities like Linhares da Beira, Belmonte, and Sortelha, where time appears to stop still. Wander through small alleyways lined with whitewashed buildings, explore old castles and fortifications, and enjoy the tranquility of country life in Beira Alta.

Beira Alta boasts stunning natural settings ideal for outdoor activities. Explore the Serra da Estrela Natural Park, which is home to Portugal's tallest mountain range and some of its most breathtaking beauty. Hike through pine forests, wander along mountain routes, and take in cascading waterfalls and crystal-clear lakes.

The Douro Valley, which forms Beira Alta's northern boundary, offers terraced vineyards, world-class wines, and gorgeous river cruises. Visit the lovely village of Lamego to ascend the renowned stairway of the Nossa Senhora dos Remédios Sanctuary and take in panoramic views of the surrounding countryside. Experience Beira Alta's rich cultural legacy by attending festivals, seeing historic places, and learning about local customs and traditions. The region has popular festivals and festivities, including the Festas de São João in Viseu, the Feira Medieval de Belmonte, and the Festa das Cruzes in Lamego.

Visit the Museum of Grao Vasco in Viseu to learn about the region's cultural legacy and see paintings by the great Portuguese painter Vasco Fernandes. Explore Belmonte's Jewish Quarter, which reflects the region's ethnic heritage, and the Jewish Museum to learn about the Jewish community's legacy in Beira Alta. Beira Alta's food highlights the region's natural riches and traditional traditions, making it a must-try for any visitor. Enjoy regional specialties, including sopa da pedra (stone soup), leitão à

Bairrada (roasted suckling pig), and queijo da Serra (Serra cheese).

Visit local markets and culinary festivals to enjoy artisanal items like honey, olive oil, and cured meats, as well as wines from the region's vineyards. Beira Alta's food reflects its cultural past and rural customs, providing a genuine flavor of Portuguese cuisine.

Beira Alta provides a range of activities for visitors interested in history, culture, nature, and food. Whether you're seeing historic sites, hiking in the mountains, or enjoying traditional food, the beauty and diversity of this wonderful area will fascinate you. Plan your stay carefully and be prepared to make experiences that will last a lifetime in Beira Alta.

MUST-SEE ATTRACTIONS AND LANDMARKS

Iconic Landmarks In Porto

Dom Luís I Bridge

This iconic double-deck metal arch bridge spans the Douro River, connecting Porto to Vila Nova de Gaia. Designed by Gustave Eiffel's student Théophile Seyrig, it offers stunning views of the city and the river below.

The Dom Luís I Bridge, which spans the Douro River and connects Porto to the scenic Vila Nova de Gaia, is an iconic feature of the city's skyline. Built in the late nineteenth century, this double-deck metal arch bridge is not only an architectural marvel, but also a treasured monument that provides breathtaking vistas and unforgettable experiences.

1. Location: The Dom Luís I Bridge connects Porto's ancient Ribeira area to the bustling shoreline of Vila Nova de Gaia by crossing the Douro River. Its central location makes it easily accessible from both sides of the river, and pedestrian paths allow tourists to explore.

2. Architectural marvel: The Dom Luís I Bridge, designed by Gustave Eiffel pupil Théophile Seyrig, is a wonder of engineering and beauty. Its ornate lattice ironwork and beautiful arches exemplify late-nineteenth century industrial beauty. The bridge's two levels—one for automotive traffic and one for pedestrians and trams—contribute to its distinctive appeal and utility.

3. Panoramic Views: The Dom Luís I Bridge offers stunning views of Porto's ancient cityscape, the Douro River, and the colorful riverbank buildings of Vila Nova de Gaia. Visitors may wander along the pedestrian walkways on both levels of the bridge to take wonderful images and appreciate the beauty of the surrounds.

4. Crossing possibilities: Explore the bridge up close with different crossing possibilities. The upper deck is allocated for pedestrians and provides uninterrupted views of the river and the metropolis. Alternatively, the lower deck supports vehicle traffic, such as autos and trams, offering a unique perspective from the center of the action.

5. Practical information:

The Dom Luís I Bridge is open 24 hours a day, so tourists may appreciate its splendor anytime.

Cost: There is no entry price to walk across the bridge, making it an affordable attraction for visitors. Visitors may walk to the Dom Luís I Bridge from several spots in Porto and Vila Nova de Gaia. Alternatively, public transit alternatives such as buses and trams offer convenient access to adjacent places.

Directed Tours: While self-directed exploration is frequent, individuals interested in learning more about the bridge's history and architecture can take a guided tour. Local tour providers give educational trips that explain its construction and importance.

The Dom Luís I Bridge represents Porto's uniqueness and human inventiveness, beyond only crossing the Douro River. Whether you're admiring its architectural magnificence, photographing panoramic vistas, or simply taking a leisurely stroll, a visit to this ancient bridge guarantees an amazing experience that will linger long after you've crossed its distinctive arches.

Ribeira District

Known for its colorful buildings, narrow streets, and bustling atmosphere, the Ribeira district is one of Porto's oldest and most picturesque neighborhoods. It's a UNESCO World Heritage Site and a popular spot for dining, shopping, and sightseeing.

The Ribeira District, located along the banks of the Douro River in Porto, Portugal, is a historic waterfront district. Ribeira is a must-see location for tourists looking to immerse themselves in the city's rich cultural heritage and energetic ambiance.

1. Ribeira District Location: is located in Porto's historic center, stretching from the Dom Luís I Bridge to the Praça da Ribeira. The central location makes it easily accessible by foot from numerous parts of the city, including prominent sites like the Sé Cathedral and São Bento Train Station.

2. Architectural Charm: The Ribeira District boasts a fascinating combination of medieval, Renaissance, and Baroque architecture, with colorful houses surrounding cobblestone lanes. Visitors may observe the ornate façade, wrought-iron balconies, and colorful azulejo tilework on the old buildings, which reflect centuries of Portuguese workmanship and artistic expression.

3. riverfront Promenade: One of the joys of seeing the Ribeira District is wandering along the riverfront promenade, which offers panoramic views of the Douro River and the renowned Dom Luís I Bridge. The promenade is dotted with outdoor cafés, restaurants, and souvenir stores, providing a lively environment that encourages people to stay and take in the sights.

4. Cultural sites: In addition to its scenic splendor, the Ribeira District has various cultural sites to explore. The Praça da Ribeira, often known as Ribeira Square, is the neighborhood's historic core and a UNESCO World Heritage site. Visitors may enjoy the fountain in the center of the plaza, sit on the stone seats, and take in the atmosphere of this vibrant public place.

5. Practical information:

Opening Hours: The Ribeira District is open 24 hours a day, so tourists may explore at their leisure. Individual businesses, restaurants, and attractions may have different operation hours.

Cost: There is no entry price to enter the Ribeira District, making it an affordable location for tourists. Visitors should plan for costs such as meals, souvenirs, and extra activities.

Getting There: The Ribeira District is easily accessible on foot from several locations across Porto's old center. Visitors may also utilize public transit, like as buses, trams, or the Funicular dos Guindais, to enjoy a lovely journey down to the river.

While self-directed exploration is popular, guided walking tours of the Ribeira District are also offered for those who want to learn more about its history, architecture, and cultural significance. Local tour providers give educational tours conducted by skilled guides who share insights into the neighborhood's history and present.

The Ribeira District is a dynamic and historic district that embodies Porto's personality and tradition. Whether you're admiring its architectural elegance, tasting traditional food at a riverfront café, or simply taking in the panoramic views of the Douro River, a visit to Ribeira guarantees an amazing experience that will wow you with its timeless beauty and attractiveness.

Sé Cathedral

Porto's imposing cathedral, Sé do Porto, is a Romanesque and Gothic masterpiece dating back to the 12th century. Visitors can admire its stunning architecture, intricate carvings, and panoramic views from the top of the bell tower.

Sé Cathedral, also known as Porto Cathedral, represents the city's religious tradition and architectural splendor. This medieval cathedral, one of Porto's oldest and most prominent structures, attracts people from all over the world due to its breathtaking beauty and rich history.

1. Sé Cathedral Location: located on a hill in Porto's historic center, offers a panoramic view of the metropolis and the Douro River. The central position allows for easy access by foot from the Ribeira District and São Bento Train Station.

2. Architectural splendor: Sé Cathedral, built in the 12th century, showcases exquisite Romanesque and Gothic styles. The massive exterior, exquisite carvings, and soaring bell towers evoke grandeur and majesty. Inside, visitors may observe the cathedral's magnificent altars, stained glass windows, and stunning barrel-vaulted roof.

3. Religious Significance: Sé Cathedral, the seat of the Bishop of Porto, is significant for both the local population and pilgrims. Its quiet interior offers a serene setting for prayer, introspection, and spiritual contemplation. Visitors can join Mass or simply see the cathedral's sacred art and antiques.

4. Practical information:

Opening Hours: Sé Cathedral is available to tourists from dawn to evening, with precise hours varied by season. To get the most up-to-date information, visit the cathedral's official website or inquire locally.

Cost: While admission to the cathedral is usually free, there may be a nominal price for entry to specific places such as the cloisters or the cathedral treasury. Donations are always welcome to help with the upkeep and preservation of this historic landmark.

Dress Code: As a place of worship, visitors to Sé Cathedral are encouraged to dress modestly, with shoulders and knees covered to honor religious traditions.

Guided excursions: While self-guided exploration is allowed, visitors interested in learning more about Sé Cathedral's history and significance can take advantage of guided excursions. Knowledgeable guides provide useful insights into the cathedral's design, artwork, and religious importance, which improves the visiting experience.

Sé Cathedral is a timeless icon of faith, history, and architectural quality in Porto. Whether you're admiring its outside architecture, marveling at its internal magnificence, or attending a prayer service, a visit to Sé Cathedral guarantees to be a remarkable and enriching experience for everyone who enters its hallowed doors.

Livraria Lello

Considered one of the most beautiful bookstores in the world, Livraria Lello is renowned for its stunning Art Nouveau architecture, grand staircase, and intricate wooden carvings. It's also famous for inspiring scenes in J.K. Rowling's Harry Potter series. Livraria Lello, often known as Lello Bookstore, is a renowned cultural institution and architectural marvel located in the heart of Porto, Portugal. Livraria Lello captivates tourists with its gorgeous Art Nouveau front, delicate woodwork interiors, and rich literary heritage.

1. *Location*: Livraria Lello is located on Rua das Carmelitas in Porto's historic center, a short walk from the busy Praça dos Leões and the University of Porto. Its central position allows for easy access by foot or public transportation, with close parking facilities for those going by vehicle.

2. Architects Xavier and Francisco Xavier Esteves created the beautiful Art Nouveau front of Livraria Lello, which has exquisite carvings, stained glass windows, and a striking crimson staircase. The inside is similarly stunning, with beautiful timber ceilings, elegant bookshelves, and fine details that convey an air of old-world luxury.

3. *Literary Legacy:* Livraria Lello left a significant literary legacy spanning over a century. It has attracted writers, intellectuals, and bibliophiles, including J.K. Rowling, who was inspired by its magical ambiance for her Harry Potter series. Today, the shop continues to promote literature with a diverse variety of books in several languages and genres.

4. *Practical information:*

Opening Hours: Livraria Lello is open everyday from morning to evening, with extended hours during high tourist season.

Admission price: To preserve the integrity of its cultural heritage and regulate tourist traffic, Livraria Lello levies an admission price. Tickets can be purchased online ahead of time or at the bookstore's door, with student, senior, and child discounts.

Guided Tours: Visitors may learn more about the history and significance of Livraria Lello through guided tours. Led by professional interpreters, these tours provide insights into the bookstore's architectural characteristics, literary links, and interesting tales from its illustrious history.

Livraria Lello is more than simply a bookshop; it's a live example of the power of literature, art, and culture. Whether you're admiring its architectural grandeur, browsing its large collection of books, or simply taking in the atmosphere of its hallowed corridors, a visit to Livraria Lello guarantees a memorable voyage into the realm of words and imagination.

Torre dos Clérigos

This iconic bell tower is part of the Clérigos Church complex and dominates Porto's skyline. Visitors can climb to the top for panoramic views of the city or explore the church and its baroque interior.

Torre dos Clérigos, often known as the Clérigos Tower, is a recognizable landmark that dominates the Porto skyline in Portugal. This Baroque bell tower, towering 76 meters tall, is not only a symbol of the city's architectural legacy, but it also provides tourists with panoramic views of Porto and its surroundings.

1. Location: Located in Porto's historic center, Torre dos Clérigos is part of the Clérigos Church complex, near the bustling Praça da Liberdade. The central position allows for easy access by foot from the Ribeira District and São Bento Train Station.

2. Torre dos Clérigos, designed by Italian architect Nicolau Nasoni in the 18th century, is a Baroque architectural masterpiece. Its exquisite design includes a cylindrical tower covered with artistic carvings, sculptures, and ornamental components, making it a visually appealing landmark that attracts tourists from far and wide.

3. Panoramic Views: At the summit of Torre dos Clérigos, visitors may enjoy panoramic views of Porto's cityscape and the Douro River. Visitors may ascend the narrow spiral staircase, which has 225 steps, to reach the observation deck, where stunning views await.

4. Practical information:

Torre dos Clérigos is available to tourists every day, with variable hours according to the season.

Torre dos Clérigos charges a small admission price, with reductions available for students, pensioners, and children. Tickets can be purchased in person or online in advance to avoid long lines during peak hours.

Climbing the Tower: Visitors should be warned that climbing Torre dos Clérigos requires navigating a small stairway with many flights of stairs. While the trek may be difficult for some, the reward of panoramic vistas at the summit is well worth it.

Guided Tours: Those interested in knowing more about Torre dos Clérigos' history and architecture can take a guided tour. These excursions, given by professional operators, provide insight into the tower's construction, history, and cultural value in Porto.

Torre dos Clérigos is a timeless icon of Porto's cultural and architectural history. Whether you're admiring its Baroque splendor, rising to its dizzying heights for panoramic views, or learning about its illustrious history on a guided tour, a visit to Torre dos Clérigos offers an amazing experience that will leave you with lasting memories of Porto's skyline.

Historic Sites In Guimarães

> ### Guimarães Castle (Castelo de Guimarães):

This medieval castle is one of Portugal's most iconic historic sites and a UNESCO World Heritage Site. Built in the 10th century, it played a significant role in the foundation of the Portuguese nation. Visitors can explore its fortified walls, towers, and interior chambers, as well as enjoy panoramic views of the city from its battlements.

> ### Ducal Palace of Guimarães (Paço dos Duques de Bragança):

Located adjacent to Guimarães Castle, this imposing palace dates back to the 15th century and served as the residence of the Dukes of Braganza. It is a fine example of Gothic architecture with Renaissance influences. Visitors can tour its elegant rooms, galleries, and gardens, which offer insight into the region's noble history and lifestyle.

> ### São Miguel do Castelo Church (Igreja de São Miguel do Castelo):

This Romanesque church is located within the walls of Guimarães Castle and dates back to the 10th century. It is one of the oldest churches in Portugal and features a simple yet beautiful interior with ancient stone carvings and artifacts.

> ### Santa Maria Street (Rua de Santa Maria):

This charming cobblestone street is lined with historic buildings dating back to the medieval period. It is considered one of the oldest streets in Guimarães and features traditional architecture, quaint shops, and cafes. Strolling along Santa Maria Street offers visitors a glimpse into the city's rich history and architectural heritage.

> ### *Oliveira Square (Largo da Oliveira):*

This picturesque square is the heart of Guimarães' historic center and is surrounded by notable landmarks such as the Church of Nossa Senhora da Oliveira and the Salado Monument. The square is named after the ancient olive tree that stands at its center and is a popular gathering place for locals and tourists alike.

Natural Wonders In Peneda-Gerês National Park

> ### *Waterfalls of Arado (Cascata do Arado):*

Located in the heart of Peneda-Gerês National Park, the Waterfalls of Arado are a series of cascades formed by the Arado River. Surrounded by lush greenery and granite cliffs, these picturesque waterfalls are a popular spot for swimming, picnicking, and hiking.

> ### *Lagoa do Gerês:*

Also known as Barragem da Caniçada, Lagoa do Gerês is a stunning reservoir nestled amidst the mountains of Peneda-Gerês National Park. Visitors can admire its crystal-clear waters, go boating or kayaking, or simply relax on its shores while enjoying the breathtaking scenery.

> ## *Tahiti Waterfall (Cascata do Tahiti):*

Hidden deep within the forested slopes of Peneda-Gerês National Park, the Tahiti Waterfall is a hidden gem waiting to be discovered. Accessible via a scenic hiking trail, this secluded cascade features a natural pool perfect for a refreshing swim.

> ## *Pedra Bela Viewpoint:*

Perched atop a rocky outcrop, Pedra Bela Viewpoint offers panoramic views of the surrounding mountains, valleys, and forests of Peneda-Gerês National Park. It's a popular spot for sunrise and sunset photography, as well as birdwatching and nature observation.

> ## *Serra do Gerês:*

The Serra do Gerês mountain range is the backbone of Peneda-Gerês National Park, offering rugged peaks, deep valleys, and pristine wilderness to explore. Hiking trails crisscross the landscape, leading to scenic viewpoints, hidden waterfalls, and remote villages where time seems to stand still.

"If you can't go to heaven, Portugal is the next best thing"

IMMERSING IN NORTHERN PORTUGUESE CULTURE

Traditional Cuisine And Gastronomy

Northern Portugal is known for its rich culinary traditions, which include a wide variety of meals that highlight the region's cultural past and local resources. Here are several must-try classic foods, including substantial stews and delicious seafood:

> ➢ **Bacalhau à Brás (Codfish à Brás):**

This traditional Portuguese meal combines salted cod, potatoes, onions, and eggs. The cod is shredded and sautéed with onions, garlic, and olive oil, then combined with thinly sliced potatoes and scrambled eggs. It's a hearty and savory dish that can be found in traditional taverns and seafood restaurants in Northern Portugal. Prices vary based on the establishment, but expect to pay between $10 and $15 each dish.

> ➢ **2. Francesinha:**

A rich and delicious sandwich that originated in Porto. It is often made out of layers of cured meats, such as ham, sausage, and steak, sandwiched between pieces of bread and drowned in a thick beer and tomato sauce. The sandwich is topped with melted cheese and comes with a side of French fries. Francesinha is a popular comfort food dish available at local cafés and restaurants, with costs ranging from $10 to $20 per serving.

> ➢ **3. Caldo Verde (Green Soup):**

This classic Portuguese soup combines kale, potatoes, onions, garlic, and chorizo. The soup is substantial and comforting, with kale providing a brilliant green color and a somewhat bitter flavor. Caldo Verde is frequently served as an appetizer or light lunch, along by crusty bread and olive oil. It's a popular dish in Northern Portugal, especially during the colder months, and can be obtained at local restaurants and pubs for $5 to $10 per bowl.

> ➢ *4. Arroz de Cabidela (Chicken Blood Rice):*

This classic Portuguese meal combines rice, chicken, and the blood of the chicken. The blood is utilized to make a rich and delicious sauce that covers the rice and chicken, providing the dish's characteristic flavor and color. Arroz de Cabidela is a popular dish during family gatherings and festivals, and it can be found in traditional taverns and restaurants around Northern Portugal. Prices vary based on the establishment, but expect to pay between $10 and $15 each dish.

> ➢ *5. Sardinha Assada (roasted Sardines):*

This popular Portuguese meal has fresh sardines roasted over an open flame. Sardines are seasoned with salt, pepper, and olive oil before grilling until soft and tasty. Sardinha Assada is a popular summer meal in Northern Portugal, where sardines are in season, and may be found at coastal cafés and seafood restaurants. Prices vary based on serving size and location, but expect to pay between $10 and $15 for a platter of grilled sardines.

Folklore And Festivals

Northern Portugal is an area rich in folklore and colorful festivals that honor its cultural history and customs. These activities, which include colorful processions as well as energetic music and dancing, provide visitors with a unique peek into the region's character. Let's explore the wonderful world of folklore and festivals in Northern Portugal, including its significance, history, and the unique experiences they provide to visitors.

> ➢ *Folklore of Northern Portugal: Preserving Tradition Through Storytelling*

Folklore is an important part of Northern Portugal's cultural identity, offering insight into the region's history and people's lives. Folk stories, legends, and myths are passed down through generations, influencing beliefs, practices, and traditions. Northern Portugal's folklore portrays its people's endurance, ingenuity, and spirit, with stories of magical woods and mythological animals, as well as love, loss, and valor.

> ➢ *Festivals of Northern Portugal: A Tapestry of Color and Celebration.*

Northern Portugal is home to a broad range of festivals honoring its religious, agricultural, and cultural past. These festivities feature vibrant processions, traditional music and dancing, ornate costumes, and delectable cuisine. Whether celebrating the harvest season, honoring patron saints, or commemorating historical events, each festival provides a unique opportunity to immerse oneself in Northern Portuguese culture and traditions.

> ### *São João Festival, Porto's Night of Fire and Fun*

The São João Festival, held yearly on June 23rd in Porto, is a well-known event in Northern Portugal. This exciting festival honors Saint John the Baptist and includes a variety of customs, such as the infamous use of plastic hammers on unsuspecting heads, the release of lit sky lanterns, and the lighting of bonfires along the Douro River. The festival's centerpiece is the midnight fireworks show, which lights up the sky in a magnificent rainbow of colors, ushering in summer with pleasure and happiness.

> ### *Romaria de São Bartolomeu: A Colorful Procession at Viana do Castelo.*

Every August, Viana do Castelo hosts the Romaria de São Bartolomeu, a celebrated celebration honoring Saint Bartholomew. The festival's highlight is the colorful procession, in which townspeople dress up in traditional costumes and parade through the streets, accompanied by music, dance, and the sound of fireworks. The celebrations also feature religious services, cultural performances, and a vibrant fair with food booths, artisan shops, and amusement rides, making it a fun festival for people of all ages.

> ### *The Feira de São Mateus is a traditional celebration in Viseu.*

The Feira de São Mateus is one of Portugal's oldest and largest fairs, dating back over 600 years. This exciting celebration, held each year in Viseu from late August to early September, commemorates Saint Matthew's feast day with a crowded marketplace, live entertainment, and cultural activities. Visitors may browse a variety of stalls offering local handicrafts, artisanal items, and regional delicacies, all while enjoying live music, folk dances, and dramatic performances that highlight Northern Portugal's rich cultural history.

> ➢ *Entrudo Chocalheiro: The Pagan Carnival of Podence.*

In the rural town of Podence, the Entrudo Chocalheiro is a one-of-a-kind carnival event that combines pagan and Christian traditions in a frenzy of color and turmoil. This historic event, held every Shrove Tuesday, sees masked revelers known as "caretos" roaming the streets, carrying cowbells and wooden poles and engaged in lighthearted mischief. The Entrudo Chocalheiro is a lively and symbolic celebration of Northern Portugal's cultural history, with the caretos representing ancient spirits thought to ward off evil and provide fertility to the land.

Folklore and festivals are central to Northern Portugal's cultural identity, providing insights into the region's rich history, customs, and beliefs. Northern Portugal's celebrations, such as São João, Romaria de São Bartolomeu, and Feira de São Mateus, showcase the resilience, creativity, and spirit of its people. As visitors experience the region's traditions and festivals, they go on a voyage of discovery and connection, creating memories that last a lifetime.

"Dear Portugal, I think about you all the time"

Arts And Crafts

Northern Portugal's arts and crafts, which range from complex azulejos to delicate filigree jewelry, demonstrate the people's creativity, talent, and cultural identities. Let's look at the various creative traditions and crafts that survive in this dynamic region, providing tourists with a unique view into its artistic essence.

➢ Azulejos: The Art Of Portuguese Tiles

Azulejos, or Portuguese tiles, are a popular style of art in Northern Portugal. These beautiful ceramic tiles, which date back to the 15th century, are known for their brilliant colors, complex patterns, and ornate designs. Azulejos decorate the facades, walls, and interiors of ancient buildings and churches, as well as public squares and individual residences, bringing beauty and appeal to the urban landscape. Visitors to Northern Portugal may see these stunning tiles in places like Porto, Braga, and Aveiro, where they stand as a living witness to the region's creative heritage.

➢ Filigree Jewelry: Exquisite Handmade Treasures

Filigree jewelry, with elaborate wirework and delicate motifs, is another defining feature of Northern Portugal's creative traditions. Artisans in locations like Gondomar and Viana do Castelo specialize in making filigree jewelry with traditions passed down through centuries. Silver and gold wires are skillfully twisted, soldered, and molded to form intricate patterns and motifs, yielding exquisite pieces of jewelry that are both elegant and ageless. Visitors may uncover these wonderful jewels by visiting local jewelry shops and artisan fairs, which sell anything from elaborately carved earrings and pendants to ornate bracelets and rings.

> ➢ **Portuguese Embroidery: A Tapestry of Tradition**

Portuguese embroidery is known for its delicate stitching, brilliant colors, and timeless motifs. Northern Portugal's Guimarães and Vila Nova de Cerveira are known for their needlework traditions, with talented artisans creating stunning works employing methods including cross-stitch, satin stitch, and bullion knot. Portuguese embroidery covers a wide range of fabrics, from table linens and bedspreads to apparel and accessories, bringing beauty and refinement into everyday life. Visitors may browse local needlework shops and craft fairs to admire and acquire these exquisitely produced pieces of art, each one a monument to the region's cultural past.

> ➢ **Ceramics: From Tradition to Innovation.**

Ceramics have long been an important component of Northern Portugal's artistic culture, with a rich history spanning centuries. In locations like Barcelos and Ílhavo, craftsmen continue to develop on traditional pottery and earthenware, including contemporary ceramics and porcelain. Visitors may visit local pottery workshops and studios to see craftspeople at work, molding clay into complex shapes and adorning them with hand painted decorations. Northern Portugal's ceramics, whether in the form of a rustic clay pot or a contemporary ceramic sculpture, celebrate creativity, craftsmanship, and tradition.

➢ Woodcarving: Maintaining the Art of Carving

Woodcarving is another beloved heritage in Northern Portugal, with craftsmen in locations like Braga and Vila Real known for their ability and workmanship. Woodcarving is a diverse art style that has been passed down through centuries, producing elaborately carved furniture and religious statues as well as ornamental panels and miniatures. Visitors may see artists at work in local woodcarving workshops, where they use traditional tools and techniques to convert wood blocks into pieces of art. Northern Portugal's woodcarvings, whether masterfully carved altarpieces or amusing folk figures, reflect the region's creative legacy and resourcefulness.

The arts and crafts of Northern Portugal represent the region's rich cultural heritage, inventiveness, and talent. From the elaborate patterns of azulejos to the delicate filigree of jewelry, each art form narrates a tale of tradition, invention, and skill. Visitors to Northern Portugal can see these creative traditions firsthand, marveling at craftsmen' talent and discovering the beauty of handcrafted goods adored for ages. Experiencing Northern Portugal's arts and crafts takes visitors on a voyage of discovery and admiration, connecting them with the people, culture, and traditions that distinguish this lively region.

"Happiness is not a state of mind, but a trip to Portugal"

COASTAL ADVENTURES

Exploring The Coastline

Northern Portugal's coastline is a treasure mine of natural beauty, cultural legacy, and undiscovered jewels. The region's coastal nature, which includes steep cliffs and sandy beaches as well as charming fishing communities and historic sites, provides a broad range of experiences for tourists seeking adventure, leisure, and discovery. Let's take a tour around Northern Portugal's coastline, discovering its numerous surprises and joys along the way.

> ### *Dramatic Cliffs of Costa Verde:*

Costa Verde, which stretches from the Minho River to the Douro River, is well-known for its rough coastline, high cliffs, and beautiful beaches. One of the most famous sites along this length of coastline is Cabo Carvoeiro, a rugged promontory near Viana do Castelo with stunning views of the Atlantic Ocean. Travelers may explore the coastal paths that zigzag along the cliffs, uncovering secret coves, sea caves, and panoramic views that highlight Northern Portugal's raw beauty.

> ### *Picturesque fishing villages:*

Northern Portugal is filled with picturesque fishing communities that provide insight into the region's marine history and way of life. One such community is Póvoa de Varzim, located on the Costa Verde, where colorful boats bob in the dock and fisherman unload their catch of the day. Visitors may walk along the beachfront promenade, sample fresh seafood at local eateries, and take in the relaxed ambiance of this historic fishing hamlet.

> ## ➤ *Surfing and Beachlife in Matosinhos:*

Matosinhos, on the northern Portuguese coast, is a must-see location for visitors looking for sun, beach, and surfing. This thriving coastal town is known for its superb surfing conditions, which draw surfers from all over the world. In addition to its gorgeous beaches, Matosinhos has a vibrant waterfront promenade dotted with cafés, bars, and seafood restaurants, making it an ideal place to unwind and enjoy the beach life vibe.

> ## ➤ *Historic Landmarks on the Costa de Prata*:

The Costa de Prata, or Silver Coast, is home to several historic sites and cultural attractions that provide insight into Northern Portugal's rich nautical heritage. The Fort of São João Baptista, situated on the island of Berlengas near Peniche, is a notable monument. This 16th-century castle is a UNESCO World Heritage site with guided tours that cover its history, architecture, and strategic importance in defending the coast from sea attackers

> ## ➤ *Explore the Douro Estuary:*

The Douro Estuary is a unique environment that supports a diverse range of bird species and marine life. Travelers may explore the estuary by boat, with guided tours that include birding, dolphin spotting, and information about the region's ecology and conservation initiatives. The estuary also has attractive cities and villages, like as Vila Nova de Gaia, where visitors may taste port wine and visit old wine cellars along the shoreline.

The craggy cliffs of Costa Verde, the sandy beaches of Matosinhos, and the ancient sites of the Costa de Prata all provide limitless options for exploration and adventure along Northern Portugal's coastline. Whether you're looking for outdoor activities, cultural events, or simply a spot to relax and appreciate nature's beauty, Northern Portugal's coastline beauties are guaranteed to fascinate and inspire. As visitors travel along this gorgeous coastline, they'll uncover a world of hidden gems and amazing experiences that will make a lasting imprint for years to come.

Beach Destinations

Northern Portugal has a diversified and attractive coastline, complete with gorgeous beaches, secret coves, and charming seaside villages. From the rocky beauty of Costa Verde to the brilliant sands of Costa de Prata, the region has a variety of beach spots to suit any traveler's preferences. Let's go on a tour to some of Northern Portugal's most beautiful beach spots, where sun, sea, and sand await.

> ➢ *Costa Verde - Rugged Beauty and Surfing Havens*

Costa Verde, often known as the Green Coast, is well-known for its rocky cliffs, untamed scenery, and superb surfing. Vila do Conde, which includes Praia de Azurara, is one of the most popular beach resorts on the Costa Verde. This lengthy expanse of golden sand is surrounded by dunes and pine woodlands, providing plenty of room for sunbathing, beach activities, and leisurely stroll down the shore. Espinho is a must-see destination for surfers, with its steady waves and strong surf culture attracting visitors from all around.

> ➢ *Costa de Prata: Golden Sands and Family-Friendly Resorts.*

The Costa de Prata, or Silver Coast, is known for its gorgeous beaches, calm waters, and family-friendly establishments. Nazaré, one of the Costa de Prata's most renowned beach resorts, is known for its huge surf and traditional fishing culture. While the north beach is known for its large waves and world-class surfing conditions, the south beach has calm seas and golden beaches ideal for swimming, sunbathing, and family trips. São Martinho do Porto's natural shell-shaped bay offers safe swimming for all ages.

> ➢ *Aveiro: Charm and Tradition on the Costa Nova*

Aveiro, often known as the "Venice of Portugal," is a delightful seaside city famed for its colorful moliceiro boats, medieval canals, and beautiful beaches. Costa Nova, a seaside community known for its striped wooden cottages and sandy beaches, is one of Aveiro's most distinctive beach attractions. Praia da Costa Nova is a popular beach destination, with broad stretches of golden sand and clean, shallow seas excellent for swimming and beach activities. Visitors may also visit the adjacent Ria de Aveiro, a breathtaking lagoon filled with wildlife and natural beauty.

> ➢ *Porto and Matosinhos provide urban beach vibes.*

Porto and its adjacent city, Matosinhos, provide urban beach getaways that mix city life with coastal beauty. Praia de Matosinhos is a popular beach recognized for its great surfing conditions, beachside eateries, and lively atmosphere. Visitors may enjoy the sun, swim in the soothing waves, or eat fresh seafood at one of the numerous beachfront eateries that along the promenade. Praia da Foz in Porto is a popular destination for both locals and visitors, with breathtaking views of the Atlantic Ocean and a famous lighthouse providing the perfect setting for a day at the beach.

The region's coastline is a treasure trove of natural beauty and coastal charm, ranging from the rugged beauty of Costa Verde to the family-friendly resorts of Costa de Prata and the urban beach vibes of Porto and Matosinhos. As tourists explore these wonderful beach resorts, they will discover a world of sun, sea, and sand that will make them want to return again and again.

Water Sports And Activities

Northern Portugal's coastline, rivers, and lakes provide numerous chances for water sports and activities, appealing to both thrill seekers and leisure aficionados. The region invites visitors to participate in exhilarating water sports ranging from surfing along the Atlantic coast to kayaking through gorgeous river basins. Let's set off on a voyage to discover the thrilling world of water sports and activities in Northern Portugal, digging into each choice with extensive information to ensure an amazing adventure.

➤ *Surfing the waves of Costa Verde*:

Costa Verde's craggy coastline provides an ideal playground for surfers of all skill levels. Praia de Azurara in Vila do Conde has regular waves and sandy bottoms that are great for novices hoping to catch their first wave. Surf schools around the coast provide instruction starting at $30 per hour, which includes board rental and a wetsuit. For experienced surfers looking for stronger swells, Espinho has world-class breaks and surf camps that provide immersive experiences for roughly $50 per session.

➤ *Kayaking through the Douro River valleys:*

Exploring the Douro River by kayak provides a unique viewpoint on Northern Portugal's breathtaking scenery and cultural history. Kayak cruises departing from Peso da Régua provide a leisurely paddle through the Douro Valley's terraced vineyards, picturesque villages, and historical sites.

Full-day guided trips are around $80 per person, which includes equipment rental and lunch. Adventurers can go on multi-day treks, sleeping along the riverbanks and immersing themselves in the area's natural splendor.

> ### Stand-Up Paddleboarding in the Minho River:

Stand-up paddleboarding (SUP) has grown in popularity along the placid waters of the Minho River, providing a relaxing opportunity to explore Northern Portugal's attractive scenery. Paddleboard rentals are offered in locations like as Caminha and Vila Nova de Cerveira, with hourly prices starting at $20, which includes the board and paddle. Guided SUP trips take paddlers through gorgeous river valleys and past old castles, offering a calm respite from the rush and bustle of city life.

> ### Windsurfing along the Atlantic Coast:

The Atlantic Ocean's high winds and rolling waves make it an ideal location for windsurfers seeking an adrenaline-fueled experience. Praia do Cabedelo, near Viana do Castelo, is well-known for its steady wind and flatwater lagoon, making it perfect for both beginners and expert windsurfers. Local surf schools rent and teach windsurfing equipment, with costs starting at $40 per hour, which includes the board, sail, and wetsuit.

> ### Canyoning at Gerês National Park:

Canyoning at Gerês National Park is a thrilling adventure set against stunning natural landscape for thrill-seekers looking for an adrenaline rush.

Canyoning excursions guide visitors through steep gorges, tumbling waterfalls, and crystal-clear pools, mixing hiking, climbing, and swimming for an exciting outdoor trip. Full-day canyoning activities at Gerês National Park start about $100 per person, which includes experienced guides, safety equipment, and transportation.

Travelers will make unforgettable memories as they immerse themselves in the natural beauty and cultural richness of Northern Portugal's aquatic treasures.

78 | Northern Portugal Travel Guide 2024

"Life is not meant to be lived in one place"

HIDDEN CHARMS AND OFF-THE-BEATEN-PATH GEMS

Quaint Villages And Rural Landscapes

As you go beyond the bustling cities and seaside villages, you'll come upon a world of timeless beauty, where old traditions meet stunning landscape. Join us on a tour across Northern Portugal's picturesque villages and rural landscapes, where every cobblestone street and rolling hill tells a story from centuries ago.

➢ *The Charm of Medieval Villages:*

Travel back in time as you explore the medieval villages that dot Northern Portugal's landscape. From the fortified walls of Belmonte to the small lanes of Sortelha, these old towns provide insight into the region's rich history and architectural legacy. Admire the well-preserved castles, cathedrals, and manor homes that serve as mute testimonies to centuries of Portuguese heritage. Take a guided walk through the cobblestone streets and discover the traditions and history that have formed these gorgeous towns into the delightful places they are today.

➢ *Tranquil rural landscapes*

Escape the hustle and bustle of city life by exploring the quiet rural landscapes that extend as far as the eye can reach. Northern Portugal is endowed with undulating hills, green valleys, and thick woods that provide a tranquil haven for nature lovers and outdoor enthusiasts alike. Lace up your hiking boots and take a magnificent hike through the Peneda-Gerês National Park, where craggy mountains, tumbling waterfalls, and crystal-clear lakes await. Alternatively, get on a bike and ride through the vineyard-covered hills of the Douro Valley, pausing to sample the region's world-renowned wines along the route.

➢ *Traditional Villages on the Douro River:*

Follow the meandering route of the Douro River through Northern Portugal's gorgeous scenery, passing by quaint villages and terraced vineyards along the way. The Douro Valley is home to some of the region's most picturesque and medieval communities, where time appears to flow at a slower pace. Discover Pinhão, a picturesque community surrounded by vineyards, with its colorful train station and charming riverfront promenade. Explore the medieval town of Lamego, which has baroque architecture and breathtaking views of the surrounding countryside. No matter where you travel, you'll be greeted with great friendliness and a sense of tranquillity found only in Northern Portugal's rural heartland.

➢ *Maintaining Traditional Ways of Life:*

Traditional ways of life continue to thrive in Northern Portugal's rural communities. Take a trip through the peaceful hamlets of the Minho area, where farmers care for their vineyards and olive groves in the same way that their forefathers did decades ago. Visit a local market to try handmade cheeses, cured meats, and freshly baked bread produced from traditions passed down through generations. Don't miss out on the chance to immerse yourself in the region's rich cultural legacy, which includes traditional festivals, folklore, and handicrafts that reflect each village's distinct personality.

As you tour Northern Portugal's small villages and rural landscapes, you'll discover a world of timeless beauty where the past and present combine effortlessly. From historic fortifications to picturesque vineyards, each stop provides insight into the region's rich history, culture, and natural beauty. Whether you're looking for peace & quiet, adventure, or just a chance to connect with the country and its people, Northern Portugal's towns and rural landscapes provide an amazing trip through the heart and soul of this magical area.

Lesser-Known Historic Sites

The Castle of Santa Maria da Feira, built in the 11th century, is one of Portugal's best-preserved specimens of medieval military construction. Visitors may tour the castle's massive walls, towers, and battlements, as well as the inner chambers and courtyard. Guided tours are provided, offering information about the castle's history and significance. Admission costs around $5 USD per person, and the castle is open everyday from 10 a.m. to 6 p.m.

Cividade de Terroso is an old fortified village near Póvoa de Varzim. This archaeological site, dating from the Iron Age, provides tourists with a look into Northern Portugal's pre-Roman culture. The site has well-preserved remains, including as stone walls, homes, and defensive constructions. Guided tours are provided, with entrance costing around $3 USD per person. The site is available to tourists from Tuesday to Sunday, 10 a.m. to 5 p.m.

The Monastery of São Pedro de Ferreira, located in the town of Ferreira near Amarante, is a hidden jewel of Romanesque architecture. Founded in the tenth century, the monastery has a basic yet graceful form that includes a central nave, apse, and cloister. Visitors may appreciate the monastery's stone sculptures, ornamental themes, and peaceful settings. Guided tours are offered upon request, and entrance is free. Visitors can visit the monastery during the week from 9 a.m. to 12 p.m. and 2 p.m. to 5 p.

The Museum and Archaeological Park of Côa Valley, located near Vila Nova de Foz Côa, houses a significant collection of prehistoric rock art in Europe. The park contains hundreds of rock carvings dating back thousands of years, featuring images of animals, humans, and abstract symbols. Visitors may explore the outdoor archeological site and learn about the region's prehistoric inhabitants via interactive displays and guided tours. Admission to the museum and park is around $10 USD per person, and opening hours vary by season.

The Castle of Lindoso, located in the Peneda-Gerês National Park, is a medieval bastion that functioned as a defense against Moorish invasions. Today, the castle is a well-preserved medieval landmark with spectacular views of the surrounding landscape. Visitors may tour the castle's towers, walls, and internal rooms, as well as the nearby hamlet with classic granite buildings and narrow cobblestone lanes. Admission to the castle is free, and it is open everyday from 9 a.m. to 6 p.m.

These lesser-known historic places provide a unique opportunity to learn about Northern Portugal's rich history and legacy, away from the throng of more renowned tourist locations. Whether seeing ancient ruins, medieval castles, or prehistoric rock art, tourists will be enthralled by the region's unique history and architectural marvels.

Scenic Drives And Hiking Trails

Northern Portugal is an outdoor enthusiast's dream, with several picturesque drives and hiking paths that highlight the region's magnificent landscapes, diversified ecosystems, and rich cultural history. Every traveler looking for adventure and discovery will find something to enjoy, from meandering seaside roads to rocky mountain pathways. Let us set out on a tour to find the most beautiful roads and hiking routes in Northern Portugal, where natural beauty greets us at every turn.

Scenic Drives:

The Douro Valley Wine Route offers a picturesque journey through terraced vineyards, charming villages, and old wine estates. The route begins in Porto and follows the Douro River as it meanders through the scenic countryside, providing breathtaking views of the valley's high hills and riverine sceneries. Visit local vineyards to taste the region's famed port wine and take leisurely stroll through picturesque villages like Pinhão and Peso do Régua.

The Serra da Estrela Scenic Drive showcases the rugged beauty of Portugal's tallest mountain range. The course starts in Guarda and rises into the highlands, passing through magnificent valleys, alpine meadows, and traditional mountain communities. The route includes stops in the medieval town of Belmonte, the glacial valleys of Manteigas, and the breathtaking scenery of the Serra da Estrela Natural Park.

Hiking trails:

Peneda-Gerês National Park offers pathways through lush woods, flowing waterfalls, and steep mountain terrain, making it ideal for hikers. The Trilho da Calcedónia is one of the park's most popular walks, following a picturesque trail along the Homem River past crystal-clear ponds and antique water mills. For more experienced hikers, the trek to Mount Gerês' top provides panoramic views of the surrounding area.

The Paiva Walkways are a network of wooden walkways and suspension bridges that connect the spectacular surroundings of the Paiva River Valley. This picturesque walk, near the town of Arouca, follows the river's winding course, providing stunning vistas of granite cliffs, lush woods, and pure waterfalls. The trail is separated into parts of varied difficulty, enabling hikers to take their favorite route while immersing themselves in the region's natural splendor.

Whether you're exploring the meandering lanes of the Douro Valley or walking through the pristine wildness of Peneda-Gerês National Park, Northern Portugal provides several possibilities to appreciate nature's grandeur up close. From panoramic views to hidden waterfalls, scenic drives and hiking paths offer a unique perspective on the region's various landscapes and cultural history. So pack your bags, hit the road, and be ready to be amazed by Northern Portugal's natural treasures.

"The best things happen outside of our comfort zones"

ACCOMMODATION OPTIONS

Luxury Hotels

➢ **Six Senses, Douro Valley**

Location: Douro Valley.

Overview: Six Senses Douro Valley, nestled among the vineyards, provides panoramic views of the river and surrounding hills. The hotel has nicely designed rooms and suites, many with their own patios. The Michelin-starred restaurant offers gourmet meals, wine tastings, and guided vineyard excursions. The spa provides a variety of revitalizing treatments with local materials. The rates start at $500 USD each night.

➢ **The Yeatman**

Location: Porto.

Overview: The Yeatman, perched on a hillside above Porto, offers exquisite rooms and suites, each with its own patio or balcony with beautiful views of the city and the Douro River. The hotel is well-known for its Michelin-starred cuisine, huge wine cellar, and wine-tasting events. Guests may relax at the Caudalie Vinothérapie Spa, which provides vinotherapy treatments using grape-based ingredients. The rates start at $400 USD each night.

➢ **Vidago Palace Hotel**

Location: Vidago

Vidago Palace Hotel is a historic luxury hotel nestled in verdant grounds, offering both traditional elegance and modern conveniences. The hotel's rooms and suites are attractively designed, with views of the surrounding gardens. Guests may take leisurely strolls around the wide grounds, play golf on the 18-hole course, or unwind with thermal spa treatments in the exquisite Vidago Palace Spa. The hotel also provides exquisite meals and afternoon tea service. The rates start at $300 USD each night.

Hotel Infante Sagres.

Hotel Infante Sagres, located in Porto's historic center, offers a blend of traditional elegance and modern amenities. The hotel's contemporary rooms and suites have plush furniture, marble baths, and modern conveniences. Guests may dine in the hotel's gourmet restaurant, sip cocktails at the trendy bar, or unwind in the quiet lounge area. The hotel also provides individual concierge service and guided tours of the city's cultural sites. Rates begin at $250 USD per night.

> ➢ *Pousada Mosteiro de Guimarães.*

Location: Guimarães.

Pousada Mosteiro de Guimarães is a magnificently renovated 12th-century convent that combines history and elegance. The hotel's large rooms and suites combine antique décor with modern facilities. Guests may eat in the hotel's gourmet restaurant, which serves traditional Portuguese cuisine, or unwind in the tranquil courtyard garden. The hotel also provides guided tours of the monastery and the city's historic core. The rates start at $200 USD each night.

Hotels And Resorts

Hotel Amares

Location: Amares.

Overview: Located in the lovely countryside of Amares, this quaint hotel provides a calm getaway surrounded by lush flora. The hotel has nice rooms and suites, a swimming pool, and a restaurant that serves traditional Portuguese cuisine. Hotel Amares is ideal for nature lovers and those seeking leisure. It offers a calm respite from the rush and bustle of daily life. Room prices begin at $100 USD per night.

Pousada Viana Do Castelo

Location: Viana do Castelo.

Overview: This old pousada overlooks the picturesque city of Viana do Castelo and the Atlantic Ocean, combining elegance and authenticity. The hotel, located in a former 16th-century convent, has beautifully refurbished rooms and suites, a gourmet restaurant, and a bar with panoramic views. Guests may visit the city's historic center, relax by the pool, or watch the sunset from the hotel's patio. Room prices begin at $150 USD per night.

Hotel Quinta do Paço de Vitorino.

Location: Guimarães.

Hotel Quinta do Paço de Vitorino is located in the heart of the Minho area and provides a serene escape surrounded by vineyards and orchards. The hotel's exquisite rooms and suites include modern conveniences and scenic views of the surrounding countryside. Guests may take a leisurely stroll around the hotel's grounds, rest by the pool, or try local wines at the on-site vineyard. Hotel Quinta do Paço de Vitorino, with its quiet environment and gorgeous setting, is ideal for a relaxing holiday. Room prices begin at $120 USD per night.

Quinta do Santo Antonio

Location: Póvoa do Lanhoso

Quinta de Santo Antonio, nestled among beautiful gardens and rolling hills, provides a tranquil retreat in the heart of Northern Portugal. The hotel's spacious rooms and suites combine rustic design with modern facilities to provide visitors with a relaxing refuge. Visitors may relax by the outdoor pool, hike the local trails, or eat regional cuisine at the on-site restaurant. Quinta de Santo Antonio is an excellent alternative for nature enthusiasts and those looking for leisure. Room prices begin at $90 USD per night.

Hotel FeelViana

Location: Viana do Castelo.

Hotel FeelViana, nestled in the breathtaking scenery of the Costa Verde, provides a one-of-a-kind combination of luxury and adventure. The hotel's contemporary rooms and villas are designed with streamlined aesthetic and eco-friendly facilities, making for a pleasant and elegant stay. Visitors may participate in a variety of outdoor sports, such as surfing, kiteboarding, and mountain biking, or relax at the spa and wellness center. Hotel FeelViana is the ideal destination for energetic visitors and outdoor lovers, thanks to its outstanding beachfront location and wealth of recreational possibilities. Room prices begin at $200 USD per night.

Hotels and resorts are the ideal starting point for discovering the region's rich culture, history, and natural beauty, thanks to their picturesque sites, pleasant amenities, and friendly service.

Bed And Breakfasts

Casa da Lage

Location: Ponte de Lima.

Casa da Lage, located in the lovely hamlet of Ponte de Lima, provides comfortable rooms in a peaceful environment. The bed & breakfast offers comfortable rooms with classic design, a shared sitting space, and a garden where visitors may unwind and enjoy the tranquil surroundings. Every morning, a full handmade breakfast is served, complete with local delicacies and fresh ingredients. Casa do Lage, with its convenient location and wonderful welcome, is an ideal refuge for those touring Northern Portugal. Prices begin at $70 USD each night.

Quinta de Galgo

Location: Vila Nova de Cerveira.

Quinta do Galgo, located in the lovely countryside near Vila Nova de Cerveira, combines rustic beauty with modern comforts. The bed & breakfast is housed in a classic Portuguese farmhouse and has comfortable guest rooms, a communal eating space, and a garden with magnificent views. Guests may begin their day with a delectable breakfast buffet with handmade bread, jams, and regional specialties. Quinta do Galgo is ideal for people seeking a tranquil escape surrounded by nature. Prices begin at $80 USD each night.

Quinta da Bouça de Arques

Location: Ponte de Lima.

Quinta da Bouça d'Arques, located in the center of Ponte de Lima and surrounded by vineyards and orchards, provides a calm respite in a historic environment. The bed & breakfast has nicely appointed rooms with vintage design, a pleasant parlor space, and a terrace that overlooks the grounds. Every morning, guests may enjoy a delightful breakfast that includes fresh fruit, pastries, and handmade jams. Quinta da Bouça d'Arques, with its tranquil setting and individual service, offers a wonderful stay for guests touring Northern Portugal. Prices begin at $90 USD each night.

Casa do Romão

Location: Amarante.

Casa de Romão, situated in the scenic village of Amarante, provides pleasant rooms in a wonderful ancient property. The bed & breakfast has attractively appointed rooms with contemporary conveniences, a comfortable parlor area with a fireplace, and a terrace with panoramic views of the surrounding landscape. Every morning, guests may enjoy a delightful breakfast with freshly baked bread, local cheeses, and handmade jams. Casa de Romão is ideal for tourists looking for a quiet retreat in a gorgeous environment. Prices begin at $100 USD each night.

Casa de Seara

Location: Vila Real.

Casa do Seara, located in the center of Vila Real, provides comfortable rooms in a renovated 18th-century home. The bed & breakfast has nicely appointed rooms with vintage design, a community eating space, and a yard filled with fruit trees and flowers. Every morning, guests may enjoy a full breakfast that includes handmade pastries, fresh fruit, and local delicacies. Casa do Seara's central position and historical charm make it an ideal base for visiting Northern Portugal. Prices begin at $110 USD each night.

These bed and breakfasts in Northern Portugal provide a warm welcome, pleasant lodgings, and individualized attention, making them a home away from home for visitors to the region. Whether tucked in the countryside or old cities, these facilities provide a unique opportunity to experience Northern Portugal's beauty and warmth.

"Good things come to those who book flights"

DINING AND CULINARY EXPERIENCES

Local Specialties And Dishes To Try

➢ *Francesinha*:

Where to buy it: Francesinha is a Porto specialty that can be found in a variety of restaurants and cafés across the city.

Cost: Prices normally range between $8 and $15 USD, depending on the restaurant and accompanying sides.

Francesinha is a hefty sandwich that consists of layers of bread, ham, linguica, and sirloin, topped with melted cheese and spicy tomato sauce. It is frequently served with french fries and a fried egg on top. Despite its name, which translates to "Little Frenchie," this meal is famous for its rich and decadent tastes, making it a must-try for visitors to Porto.

➢ **Caldo Verde:**

Caldo Verde is a typical Portuguese soup available at restaurants and taverns across Northern Portugal.

Cost: Prices for bowls normally vary between $5 and $10 USD, depending on the venue and accompanying bread.

Overview: Caldo Verde is a hearty soup prepared with potatoes, kale, onions, garlic, and chorizo or linguica sausage. It's cooked until the flavors combine, creating a substantial and savory meal ideal for winter evenings. Caldo Verde, served with crusty bread, is a Portuguese culinary classic that is popular with both residents and visitors.

> ### Bacalhau á Brás:

Where to acquire it: Bacalhau à Brás is available in traditional Portuguese restaurants across Northern Portugal, especially in seaside areas.

Cost: Prices normally range between $10 and $20 USD, depending on meal size and establishment.

Overview: Bacalhau à Brás is a traditional Portuguese meal prepared from salted fish, onions, potatoes, and eggs. The fish is shredded and sautéed with onions and garlic until golden brown, then combined with scrambled eggs and shoestring potatoes. The meal is tasty and fulfilling, with the right amount of saltiness from the fish and richness from the eggs. It is frequently served with a side salad or olives to complete the meal.

> ### Arroz de Pato

Where to buy it: Arroz de Pato is a popular meal in Northern Portugal, particularly in Porto and Braga.

Prices for a single plate normally range between $15 and $25 USD, depending on the restaurant and accompanying sides.

Overview: Arroz de Pato is a rich and savory classic Portuguese duck rice dish. Soft duck flesh is sautéed with rice, chorizo, onions, and garlic, then baked until the rice is soft and the flavors have combined. The meal is frequently topped with chorizo and served with orange slices on the side, which give a zesty sweetness to each bite. Arroz de Pato is a hearty and pleasant dish ideal for sharing with family and friends.

> ➤ *Pastel de Nata*

Where to purchase it: Pastel de Nata may be found at bakeries and cafés across Northern Portugal, with some of the most well-known locations in Porto and Lisbon.

Cost: Prices for pastries normally vary from $1 to $3 USD, depending on size and quality.

Overview: Pastel de Nata, often known as Portuguese custard tart, is a renowned dish that originated in Lisbon but has spread throughout Portugal. These flaky pastry shells are filled with a rich and creamy custard of eggs, sugar, and milk then baked until the tops are caramelized and somewhat blistered. The end product is a delectably sweet and creamy dessert that pairs perfectly with a cup of coffee or tea. Pastel de Nata is a must-try for anybody visiting Northern Portugal who likes sweets.

Top Restaurants And Eateries

➤ **DOP Restaurant**

Location: Rua do Padre Luís Cabral 31, Porto.

Opening hours: Tuesday through Saturday, 12:30 PM to 3:00 PM and 7:30 PM to 11:00 PM; closed Sundays and Mondays.

Overview: DOP Restaurant, located in the center of Porto, serves a modern spin on classic Portuguese food. Chef Rui Paula uses the freshest ingredients from Northern Portugal to create unique and tasty meals. The restaurant's exquisite dining room offers a refined atmosphere for customers to savor specialties such as Bacalhau à Brás and Roasted Suckling Pig. DOP Restaurant is popular with both residents and visitors due to its exceptional service and inventive culinary choices.

➤ *Pedro Lemos Restaurant*

Location: Rua do Padre Luís Cabral 974, Porto.

Opening hours: Tuesday through Saturday, 12:30 PM to 3:00 PM and 7:30 PM to 11:00 PM; closed Sundays and Mondays.

Overview: Pedro Lemos Restaurant, located in Porto's Foz do Douro area, is well-known for its unique approach to Portuguese food. Chef Pedro Lemos mixes classic tastes with modern techniques to produce dishes that are both visually appealing and appetizing. Octopus Carpaccio and Black Pork Belly are among the highlights of the restaurant's tasting menus, which take diners on a gastronomic trip around Northern Portugal. Pedro Lemos Restaurant provides an amazing dining experience because of its exquisite setting and meticulous attention to detail.

> ➤ **Restaurante Largo do Paço**

Location: Largo do Paço, 6, Amarante.

Daily hours are 12:30 PM to 3:00 PM and 7:30 PM to 10:30 PM.

Overview: Restaurante Largo do Paço, located inside the ancient Casa da Calçada Relais & Châteaux hotel in Amarante, serves excellent Portuguese cuisine in a luxury environment. Grilled Sea Bass and Roast Lamb are two meals prepared by Chef Tiago Bonito that highlight the best products from the region. The restaurant's magnificent dining room has vaulted ceilings and antique furnishings, creating an attractive setting for a wonderful dining experience. Restaurante Largo do Paço is Northern Portugal's culinary treasure, with great service and exquisite cuisine.

> ➤ **Tasca de Esquina**

Location: Rua de São Paulo 84, Porto.

Opening hours: Tuesday through Saturday, 12:30 PM to 3:00 PM and 7:30 PM to 11:00 PM; closed Sundays and Mondays.

Overview: Tasca da Esquina is a charming neighborhood restaurant in Porto's Ribeira area recognized for its friendly service and delectable Portuguese cuisine. Chef Vítor Sobral produces seasonal dinners influenced by traditional tastes, such as Codfish Fritters and Braised Beef Cheeks. The restaurant's informal atmosphere and courteous service make it a popular choice for both residents and visitors seeking traditional Portuguese food in a comfortable environment.

> ### *Restaurante a Cozinha*

Location: Largo do Paço 6, Guimarães.

Opening hours are Tuesday through Sunday, 12:30 PM to 3:00 PM and 7:30 PM to 11:00 PM; closed on Mondays.

Overview: Restaurante A Cozinha in Guimarães serves contemporary Portuguese food in a sophisticated atmosphere. Chef António Loureiro highlights the region's tastes in dishes such as Octopus with Sweet Potato Purée and Roast Duck Breast. The restaurant's sleek dining area boasts a modern design and panoramic views of the city, giving an attractive setting in which customers can enjoy a memorable dinner. Restaurant A Cozinha is a must-see location in Northern Portugal, thanks to its innovative food and breathtaking environment.

These restaurants in Porto, Amarante, and Guimarães provide great food, service, and amazing dining experiences.

PRACTICAL TRAVEL TIPS
Language And Communication

Northern Portugal, like the rest of the nation, is largely Portuguese-speaking. Visitors should be aware of the region's distinctive language traits and communication traditions.

Northern Portugal has numerous different Portuguese dialects, each with unique qualities and subtleties. In places like Porto and Braga, you may notice differences in pronunciation, vocabulary, and grammar from standard Portuguese. While most residents understand and speak standard Portuguese, it is not unusual to hear regional dialects and phrases in daily speech.

Mirandese is a language spoken in Northern Portugal, namely in the Miranda do Douro region, together with Portuguese. Mirandese is recognized as a co-official language with Portuguese, and it is spoken by a small but considerable number of people in the region. Visitors may come across signage, literature, and cultural events in Mirandese, demonstrating the linguistic variety of Northern Portugal.

Northern Portuguese communication style emphasizes warmth, friendliness, and hospitality. Locals are typically warm and accommodating to guests, and a simple "Bom dia" (good morning) or "Obrigado" (thank you) can help build rapport. Hand gestures and nonverbal clues are frequently employed in discussions to communicate ideas and express emotions.

English Proficiency: While Portuguese is the major language spoken in Northern Portugal, many residents, especially in metropolitan regions and tourist sites, are proficient in English. Hotel employees, restaurant servers, and tour guides frequently speak English to assist foreign guests. However, outside of major tourist destinations, English competence may be limited, so knowing some basic Portuguese words might aid in communication.

When engaging with natives in Northern Portugal, it's important to respect cultural sensitivity and norms. Respect for elders, civility, and personal space are highly prized in Portuguese culture. It is generally courteous to address somebody with "senhor" (Mr.) or "senhora" (Mrs.), followed by their last name. Furthermore, learning a few simple Portuguese phrases, such as greetings and appreciation, indicates cultural sensitivity and improves the whole vacation experience.

language and communication in Northern Portugal reflect the country's vast linguistic variety and cultural legacy. While Portuguese is the major language spoken, travelers may come across regional dialects, including the Mirandese language, in some locations. Understanding the local communication style, English proficiency levels, and cultural sensitivity can help tourists negotiate encounters and immerse themselves more deeply in Northern Portugal's colorful culture.

Travel Phrases For Northern Portugal

➢ *Greetings:*

"Bom dia" - Good morning

"Boa tarde" - Good afternoon

"Boa noite" - Good evening / Good night

"Olá" - Hello

"Tudo bem?" - How are you?

"Obrigado/a" - Thank you (male/female)

"Por favor" - Please

➢ *Basic Conversations:*

"Fala inglês?" - Do you speak English?

"Eu não falo português" - I don't speak Portuguese

"Pode me ajudar?" - Can you help me?

"Qual é o seu nome?" - What is your name?

"Eu sou turista" - I am a tourist

"Eu gostaria de..." - I would like to...

"Onde fica o banheiro?" - Where is the bathroom?

➢ *Getting Around:*

"Onde é a estação de trem/ônibus?" - Where is the train/bus station?

"Quanto custa o bilhete?" - How much is the ticket?

"Para o aeroporto, por favor" - To the airport, please

"Pode chamar um táxi para mim?" - Can you call a taxi for me?

"Estou perdido/a" - I am lost

"Qual é a melhor maneira de chegar lá?" - What is the best way to get there?

➤ *Dining Out:*

"Mesa para dois, por favor" - Table for two, please

"O menu, por favor" - The menu, please

"Eu sou vegetariano/a" - I am vegetarian

"Recomendação do chef" - Chef's recommendation

"A conta, por favor" - The bill, please

"Aceita cartão de crédito?" - Do you accept credit cards?

➤ *Emergencies:*

"Preciso de ajuda" - I need help

"Chame uma ambulância / polícia" - Call an ambulance / police

"Perdi os meus documentos" - I lost my documents

"Estou doente" - I am sick

"Onde é o hospital mais próximo?" - Where is the nearest hospital?

"Estou a ser assaltado/a" - I am being robbed

Learning these phrases can greatly enhance your travel experience in Northern Portugal and help you navigate various situations with ease and confidence.

Safety And Health Considerations

> ### General Safety Precautions:

Northern Portugal is regarded as a safe tourist destination, with crime rates lower than in many other European nations. However, visitors should use common sense and take simple steps to protect their safety.

Stay watchful in crowded tourist areas and be wary of pickpockets, especially in big towns like Porto and Braga. Keep your stuff safe and avoid exhibiting precious goods openly. Be cautious when visiting new places, especially at night. Stick to well-lit streets and avoid going alone in remote locations. Familiarize yourself with local emergency numbers, such as 112 for general emergencies and 144 for medical situations.

Health precautions:

Northern Portugal boasts a well-developed healthcare system, with hospitals and medical facilities located in major cities and villages. Pharmacies (farmácias) are widely available and can supply over-the-counter drugs as well as general medical advice.

Travelers should have adequate travel insurance that covers medical emergencies and repatriation.

Tap water in Northern Portugal is typically safe to drink, however, bottled water is easily accessible for those who want it. Northern Portugal has a temperate temperature, but tourists should still take measures to avoid sunburn and dehydration, particularly during the summer months. Use sunscreen, remain hydrated, and seek shade during the warmest hours of the day.

If you have any special health issues or need prescription medicine, you should check with a healthcare physician before going to ensure you have enough supplies and information.

Outdoor Safety:

Northern Portugal has spectacular natural scenery and outdoor leisure options, such as hiking, riding, and water sports. However, vacationers should use caution when participating in outdoor activities. Dress correctly for the weather and terrain, wear strong footwear, and bring necessary supplies like water, food, and a map or GPS device. Before heading out, check local weather predictions and trail conditions, and be prepared for weather fluctuations, particularly in hilly places.

By following these safety and health precautions, tourists may have a fulfilling and memorable trip in Northern Portugal while emphasizing their well-being and peace of mind.

Currency And Banking

Currency:

Portugal's official currency is the Euro (€), abbreviated EUR. It is widely used in Northern Portugal for all transactions, including shopping, meals, and lodging. The Euro is divisible into 100 cents, and coins come in denominations of 1, 2, 5, 10, 20, and 50 cents, as well as €1 and €2 coins. Banknotes come in denominations of €5, €10, €20, €50, €100, €200, and €500.

ATMs (Automated Teller Machines) are widely distributed across Northern Portugal, particularly in metropolitan areas and tourist sites. They accept major international credit and debit cards, including Visa, MasterCard, and American Express, as well as Euros.

Bank Hours:

Banking hours in Northern Portugal normally run from Monday to Friday, with occasional variances depending on the institution. Most banks are open from 8:30 a.m. to 3:00 p.m., with a lunch break occurring between 1:00 and 2:00 p.m. Some banks may also be open on Saturday mornings however, this varies by area.

It is recommended that you check the opening hours of certain banks or branches ahead of time since they may vary based on location and local customs.

Currency Exchange:

Currency exchange services are offered in banks, currency exchange offices (cambios), and some hotels in major towns and tourist destinations. While converting money at banks is typically dependable, you should check exchange rates and fees to verify you're receiving the best price. Avoid converting money at airports or tourist areas since the rates may be less advantageous.

Many businesses in Northern Portugal, particularly those that cater to visitors, accept major credit and debit cards. However, it is still recommended to carry cash for minor purchases and transactions in more distant places.

Payment methods:

Credit and debit cards are commonly accepted across Northern Portugal, particularly in metropolitan areas and tourist sites. The most often accepted cards are Visa and MasterCard, followed by American Express and Diners Club International. Contactless payments are gaining popularity in Portugal, enabling quick and easy transactions for modest purchases.

It's best to notify your bank of your trip intentions before leaving to avoid any problems with card usage overseas, such as surprise declines or fraud alerts.

Traveler's checks:

Traveler's checks are less popular in Northern Portugal than in the past, and many places may not take them. For ease and flexibility on your trips, bring a combination of cash and credit cards.

You can manage financial transactions with comfort and easily during your stay in Northern Portugal if you are familiar with the local currency and banking processes.

"Born to explore the world"

CULTURAL ETIQUETTE AND CUSTOMS

Dos And Don'ts For Travelers

Dos:

➢ **Do learn basic Portuguese phrases**.

While many people in Northern Portugal understand English, learning simple Portuguese words like hello, please, and thank you can improve your trip experience and demonstrate respect for the local culture.

➢ **Do respect the local customs and traditions.**

Northern Portugal has a rich cultural heritage and practices that are strongly embedded in society. To prevent offending someone accidentally, respect local norms such as dining manners, religious beliefs, and personal space.

➢ **Do explore beyond the tourist hotspots.**

While renowned cities such as Porto and Braga are must-sees, don't be afraid to wander off the beaten path and discover smaller towns and villages in Northern Portugal. You will uncover hidden jewels, real experiences, and a stronger connection to the local culture.

➢ **Do Embrace Culinary Delights**

Northern Portugal is well-known for its superb gastronomy, which includes fresh fish, substantial stews, and pastries. Try local favorites like bacalhau (salted fish), Francesinha (a substantial sandwich), and pastéis de nata (custard tarts) at authentic restaurants and marketplaces.

> ### ➤ *Do practice responsible tourism.*

Practicing responsible tourism can help to preserve Northern Portugal's natural beauty and cultural legacy. Respect protected areas, use established routes and properly dispose of rubbish to reduce your environmental effect.

Don'ts:

> ### ➤ *Do not expect dinner before 8:00 p.m.*

Dinner in Northern Portugal is usually served later in the evening, at 8:00 p.m. or later. To avoid disappointment, plan your meals around local customs.

> ### ➤ *Do not forget to validate your train ticket.*

If you're going by rail in Northern Portugal, make sure you confirm your ticket before boarding. Failure to do so may result in fines, so locate the validation devices on the platform and stamp your ticket before leaving.

> ### ➤ *Do not overlook safety precautions:*

While Northern Portugal is largely secure for tourists, use care in crowded tourist locations and be wary of pickpocketing and petty theft. Keep valuables protected and stay attentive to your surroundings, especially in congested metropolitan areas.

➤ Do Not Underestimate the Terrain:

Northern Portugal's various landscapes provide several chances for outdoor activities such as hiking and exploration. However, do not underestimate the terrain, particularly in hilly areas. Always pack suitable footwear, clothes, and materials for outdoor trips.

➤ *Do not be afraid to ask for help.*

If you have any queries or require assistance when traveling in Northern Portugal, please do not hesitate to ask. Locals are typically polite and hospitable to visitors, and they will frequently go out of their way to provide you with directions, advice, or information.

By following these dos and don'ts for Northern Portugal visitors, you may maximize your vacation while respecting local customs, increasing your safety, and creating great experiences in this intriguing area.

"Eat well, travel often"

SHOPPING AND SOUVENIRS

Local Crafts And Products

Northern Portugal is known for its rich cultural legacy and traditional craftsmanship, which provides tourists with a diverse range of unique and original things to discover and purchase. From handcrafted pottery to gorgeous fabrics, the region has a thriving artisanal scene that reflects its history, culture, and natural environment.

> ➢ *Portuguese ceramics:*

Ceramics are one of Northern Portugal's most recognized handmade traditions. From delicately painted tiles (azulejos) to brilliantly glazed ceramics, the region's ceramic artists create a diverse range of ornamental and practical pieces.

Visit ceramic workshops and studios in places like Porto, Guimarães, and Barcelos to see craftsmen at work and acquire unique gifts.

> ➢ *Textile and embroidery:*

Northern Portugal is well known for its gorgeous fabrics and sophisticated needlework skills. From handmade blankets and rugs to beautifully embroidered linens and outfits, the region's textile artists demonstrate outstanding skill and attention to detail.

Textile museums and artisanal stores in locations such as Braga and Viana do Castelo allow visitors to observe ancient textile processes while also purchasing high-quality fabrics and needlework goods directly from local craftspeople.

> ## *Portuguese Pottery and Tiles:*

For millennia, pottery and tile manufacturing have been an intrinsic part of Northern Portugal's cultural history. Artisans in towns such as Porto and Aveiro create magnificent hand-painted tiles (azulejos) and ornate ceramics using ancient skills passed down through centuries.

Visitors may tour ceramic tile manufacturers and pottery workshops, learn about the history of Portuguese tile manufacturing, and buy one-of-a-kind tiles and pottery pieces to decorate their homes.

> ## *Port Wine and Cork Products:*

Northern Portugal is well-known for its port wine, which is only made in the Douro Valley. Visitors may tour vineyards and wine cellars in Porto and the Douro Valley, sampling a range of port wines and purchasing bottles to take home.

Portugal is also the world's largest producer of cork, and tourists may discover a variety of cork goods, such as purses, wallets, and accessories, at stores around Northern Portugal.

> ## *Traditional Wood Crafts:*

Wooden crafts are especially popular in Northern Portugal, where artists create a wide range of hand-carved goods such as furniture, kitchenware, and ornamental things. Woodworking businesses and artisanal marketplaces in locations like Braga and

Guimarães provide unique wooden objects manufactured with ancient techniques.

Visitors may immerse themselves in Northern Portugal's rich cultural history and support local craftsmen by discovering the region's native crafts and goods, as well as bringing home unique and original souvenirs that will serve as lasting mementos of their trip.

Markets And Shopping Districts

Northern Portugal has a rich and active retail environment, with bustling markets and lovely shopping areas where tourists can discover a variety of local items, handmade crafts, and one-of-a-kind souvenirs. From ancient markets to sophisticated retail malls, the region caters to all interests and inclinations, giving guests an unforgettable shopping experience.

➤ *Mercado do Bolhão in Porto:*

Mercado do Bolhão, located in the center of Porto, is a traditional and renowned market. This lively market, which dates back to the nineteenth century, is well-known for its colorful ambiance and broad selection of fresh fruit, meats, fish, and local specialties.

Visitors may browse the market's vibrant booths, chat with local merchants, and try regional delicacies like Porto's famed smoked sausages (chouriços) and artisanal cheeses. Mercado do Bolhão includes handicrafts, fabrics, and souvenirs, making it a popular shopping location.

➤ *Rua da Santa Catarina, Porto:*

Rua de Santa Catarina is Porto's main shopping route, containing a mix of traditional businesses, foreign brands, and locally owned boutiques. This bustling avenue provides a diverse shopping experience, including fashion and accessories, gourmet food outlets, and craft businesses.

Visitors may shop for unique products and souvenirs at prominent locations like the historic Café Majestic and the exquisite Via Catarina Shopping Mall. Rua de Santa Catarina also hosts frequent street performers and cultural events, which contribute to its vibrant atmosphere.

➤ *Braga's Municipal Market (Mercado Municipal de Braga)*

Braga Municipal Market is a thriving indoor market in the heart of Braga's historic district. This lively market is open every day and serves as a focus of activity, offering a diverse assortment of fresh fruit, meats, cheeses, and local specialties derived from the surrounding area.

In addition to its fresh food options, Braga Municipal Market has kiosks selling traditional handicrafts, textiles, and souvenirs, allowing tourists to find original local items while immersed in the city's cultural legacy.

➤ *Shopping City of Porto (Porto City Shopping), Porto:*

Retail Cidade do Porto is one of Porto's main retail complexes, providing a modern and diversified shopping experience. This wide mall near the city center houses a diverse assortment of stores, including fashion boutiques, electronics merchants, and department stores.

Visitors may buy from worldwide brands and designer labels, eat at a variety of restaurants and cafés, watch movies, and play arcade games. Shopping Cidade do Porto offers a simple and enjoyable shopping experience for guests who want to engage in retail therapy.

> ➢ **Avenida dos Aliados in Porto**:

Avenida dos Aliados is Porto's magnificent thoroughfare, lined with fine buildings, stores, and cafés. This landmark street is a popular shopping destination, with a mix of luxury boutiques, souvenir shops, and specialty businesses.

Visitors may meander around Avenida dos Aliados, enjoying the architecture and shopping for one-of-a-kind goods and souvenirs. The Boulevard also holds seasonal markets and cultural events, which contribute to its appeal as a retail and entertainment destination.

Visitors to Northern Portugal's markets and shopping areas may find a multitude of local items, handcrafted crafts, and one-of-a-kind souvenirs while immersed in the region's colorful culture and tradition. Northern Portugal provides a memorable shopping experience for all visitors, whether they are looking for fresh food in a traditional market or indulging in retail therapy at a sophisticated shopping mall.

"When in doubt, just travel"

NIGHTLIFE AND ENTERTAINMENT

Bars And Clubs

➤ **Praça da Ribeira in Porto:**

Praça da Ribeira is a lovely square in Porto's old Ribeira area that overlooks the Douro River.

Overview: Praça da Ribeira is renowned for its bustling ambiance and active nightlife scene. The area is dotted with traditional taverns, pubs, and cafés, where tourists may enjoy a range of beverages and local dishes while taking in the picturesque riverfront setting. Many places have outside dining, making it ideal for a relaxing evening of people-watching and mingling.

Opening hours: Bars and cafes in Praça da Ribeira often open in the late afternoon and stay open until early in the morning, especially on weekends and during busy tourist seasons.

➤ **Galeries de Paris, Porto:**

Galerias de Paris is a vibrant nightlife sector in the center of Porto's city, next to Avenida dos Aliados.

Overview: Galerias de Paris is known for its varied mix of pubs, clubs, and entertainment venues, making it a popular destination for both locals and tourists. The region has a wide range of entertainment alternatives, from fashionable cocktail bars to intense dance clubs, appealing to a variety of interests and inclinations. Visitors may expect a lively environment, live music performances, and a throng of partygoers enjoying the active nightlife scene.

Opening Hours: Bars and clubs in Galerias de Paris usually open in the evening and stay open until early in the morning, especially on weekends and for special occasions.

> ### ➤ *Largo de São Domingos, Braga.*

Largo de São Domingos is a lovely area in Braga's old center, with classic cafés and pubs.

Overview: Largo de São Domingos provides a more casual and laid-back nightlife experience than major towns like Porto. The area is lined with quaint cafés and restaurants where tourists can relax with a drink and soak up the local atmosphere. Largo de São Domingos offers a cozy atmosphere for mingling and leisure, whether you're drinking wine or trying regional artisan brews.

Bars and cafés in Largo de São Domingos are often open from late afternoon to late evening, serving both daytime and evening guests.

> ### ➤ *Rua das Galerias in Vila Nova de Gaia:*

Rua das Galerias is a bustling street in Vila Nova de Gaia, across the Douro River from Porto's historic center.

Overview: Rua das Galerias is home to a broad range of bars, pubs, and nightlife places, providing tourists with a vibrant and energetic ambiance. From classic Portuguese taverns to trendy cocktail bars, the street caters to a diverse spectrum of interests and inclinations. Visitors to this lively nightlife hotspot may enjoy a range of beverages, live music performances, and DJ sets while socializing with locals and fellow visitors.

Opening Hours: Bars and bars on Rua das Galerias normally open in the evening and stay open until early in the morning, particularly on weekends and during holidays.

> ➢ *Praça da República in Viana do Castelo:*

Praça da República is a significant square in Viana do Castelo, a picturesque seaside town in Northern Portugal.

Overview: Praça da República is a popular gathering location for residents and visitors, offering a range of pubs and cafés to rest and unwind. The square's historic environs, especially the landmark Paços do Concelho (Town Hall), make an idyllic setting for an evening of drinks and mingling. Praça da República provides a peaceful and friendly ambiance for nightlife aficionados, whether they enjoy a refreshing beverage on a patio or sample local delicacies in a snug pub.

Bars and cafes in Praça da República often open in the late afternoon and stay open until late evening, allowing tourists to experience the town's nightlife attractions.

Each of these pubs and clubs provides a distinct ambiance and experience, guaranteeing that visitors to Northern Portugal may choose the ideal location for a fantastic night out.

Live Music Venues

> ➤ **Casa da Música in Porto:**

Casa da Música, a contemporary music venue in Porto's Boavista area, was created by famous architect Rem Koolhaas.

Overview: Casa da Música is a premier live music venue in Porto, featuring a varied range of events such as classical concerts, jazz ensembles, current music, and world music artists. The venue's remarkable architectural design and cutting-edge acoustics ensure that fans have an immersive and unforgettable musical experience. Casa da Música provides guided tours, educational events, and seminars, making it a cultural magnet for music lovers of all ages.

Opening Hours: Opening hours change according to the scheduled performances and activities. Visitors may consult the venue's calendar for the most up-to-date musical schedule and ticket availability.

> ➤ **Hard Club, Porto:**

Hard Club is a well-known live music venue located in Porto's old Ribeira area, overlooking the Douro River.

Overview: Hard Club is a popular location for live music fans, with a diverse program of concerts encompassing rock, indie, electronic, and alternative music. The venue's industrial-chic decor and compact ambiance provide an immersive environment in which both local and international performers may display their abilities. In addition to live music performances, Hard Club provides DJ sets, club nights, and cultural events, making it a popular nightlife spot in Porto.

Opening Hours: The Hard Club is usually open at night, with concerts and activities booked throughout the week. Doors open about an hour before the planned showtimes.

> ### Theatro Circo, Braga:

Theatro Circo is a historic theater in the heart of Braga's city center, close to the famed Avenida da Liberdade.

Overview: Theatro Circo is well-known for its rich cultural legacy and diverse programming, which includes theater productions, dance events, concerts, and musical performances. The venue's opulent interior and beautiful architecture create a grand setting for live music performances, attracting visitors from all across the region. Theatro Circo also conducts cinema screenings, art exhibitions, and community activities, making it a thriving cultural center in Braga.

Opening Hours: Theatro Circo's operating hours change according to booked acts and activities. Visitors can check the venue's website or box office for details on future concerts and ticket availability.

> ### Centro Cultural Vila Flor in Guimarães:

Centro Cultural Vila Flor is located in Guimarães, a UNESCO World Heritage Site.

Overview: Centro Cultural Vila Flor is a multifunctional cultural complex that showcases a wide range of creative and musical activities, such as concerts, theatrical shows, dance recitals, and multimedia works. The venue's contemporary amenities and adaptable areas can host a variety of events, ranging from small chamber music concerts to large-scale performances by renowned performers. Centro Cultural Vila Flor also provides educational programs, artist residencies, and cultural projects that strengthen the local arts scene while encouraging creativity and innovation.

Opening Hours: Centro Cultural Vila Flor's operating hours change based on the scheduled activities and exhibitions. Visitors are invited to visit the venue's website or call the box office for details on future performances and ticket availability.

> ➢ **Plan B, Porto:**

Plano B is a bustling nightlife location in Porto's central district, next to the historic Lello Bookstore.

Overview: Plano B is well-known for its diversified roster of live music performances, DJ sets, and cultural events, which draws a diverse population of music fans and partygoers. The venue's underground ambiance and compact location create an immersive experience for fans, with performances ranging from indie rock bands to electronic music groups. Plano B also offers themed parties, art exhibitions, and film screenings, making it a popular nightlife and entertainment venue in Porto.

Plano B is normally open at night, with live music and activities planned throughout the week. Doors open about an hour before the planned showtimes.

These live music venues provide an interesting and diverse range of concerts, giving visitors to Northern Portugal unforgettable experiences and opportunities to learn about the region's lively music industry.

Cultural Performances

Visitors to the region may immerse themselves in Northern Portugal's active cultural scene, which includes folk music, dance, theater, and art exhibitions.

➢ Folk Music and Dance Festivals:

Throughout the year, Northern Portugal stages a number of folk music and dance events that honor the region's cultural heritage. These events highlight traditional music genres like fado, ranchos folclóricos, and cantares ao desafio, with performances by local musicians and dancing troupes costumed in vibrant costumes. Visitors may enjoy the bright rhythms and captivating energy of Portuguese folk music while also learning about the region's cultural history.

➢ Theater & Performance Arts:

Northern Portugal is home to various theaters and performing arts institutions that host a wide range of theatrical events, such as plays, musicals, and experimental performances. Theatergoers may enjoy a variety of performances in tiny black box theaters, historic playhouses, and modern cultural facilities, including classic plays and contemporary pieces by local authors. These performances delve into Portuguese culture, history, and society, presenting spectators with thought-provoking and engaging experiences.

➢ Art Exhibitions and Cultural Events:

Art galleries, museums, and cultural organizations around Northern Portugal hold a wide range of art exhibitions and cultural activities that promote the region's artistic skill and creative expression. Visitors may explore modern art installations, photography displays, and sculpture gardens, as well as participate in artist talks, workshops, and film screenings. These cultural events promote cultural interchange and debate, resulting in a better knowledge and appreciation of Northern Portugal's creative history.

> ➤ ***Traditional festivals and celebrations:***

Northern Portugal is well-known for its vivid traditional and cultural festivals, which take place year-round in villages, towns, and cities throughout the area. Religious processions and patron saint festivals, as well as seasonal harvest festivities and local fairs, provide insight into Northern Portuguese towns' customs, rituals, and culture. Visitors may take part in traditional dances, sample regional specialties, and watch centuries-old customs being kept and passed down through generations.

> ➤ ***Street performance and cultural parades:***

In addition to organized cultural events and performances, Northern Portugal's streets are alive with spontaneous street performances, cultural parades, and outdoor shows. Visitors to public areas may enjoy the energy and inventiveness of Portuguese culture through impromptu musical performances and street art projects, as well as colorful parades and processions. These street performances allow for connection and participation with local artists and performers, resulting in unforgettable experiences and lasting memories.

Overall, cultural performances in Northern Portugal provide tourists with a unique and rewarding experience by highlighting the region's cultural history, artistic expression, and community spirit. Visitors may immerse themselves in Northern Portugal's vibrant cultural tapestry by visiting a folk music festival, touring an art exhibition, or watching a traditional procession.

"My favorite thing is to go where I've never been"

DAY TRIPS AND EXCURSIONS

Nearby Destinations Worth Visiting

> ➤ **Douro Valley:**

The Douro Valley, located only a short drive from Porto, is well-known for its breathtaking scenery, terraced vineyards, and world-class winemaking. Visitors may enjoy breathtaking boat rides down the Douro River, see old wine farms known as quintas, and sip superb port wines in picturesque riverside villages like Pinhão and Peso da Régua.

> ➤ **Guimarães:**

Guimarães, dubbed the "birthplace of Portugal," is a historic city with medieval charm and cultural significance. Highlights include the UNESCO-listed Guimarães Castle, the majestic Palace of the Dukes of Braganza, and the charming lanes of the old city center. Visitors may immerse themselves in the dynamic ambiance of the city while learning about its rich history, architecture, and local food.

> ➤ **Braga:**

Braga is a bustling city recognized for its religious heritage, Baroque architecture, and vibrant cultural scene. Visitors may visit the magnificent Bom Jesus do Monte Sanctuary, view the old Sé Cathedral, and walk through the city's lovely streets. Braga also holds a number of cultural events, festivals, and markets throughout the year, giving visitors plenty of possibilities to explore and discover.

> ## *Aveiro:*

Aveiro, sometimes known as the "Venice of Portugal," is a gorgeous seaside city with colorful moliceiro boats, Art Nouveau buildings, and attractive canals. Visitors may enjoy a leisurely boat cruise around the canals, try classic Portuguese pastries known as ovos moles, and visit the lively fish market at the Mercado do Peixe. Aveiro's closeness to beautiful beaches and environmental areas makes it an excellent choice for outdoor enthusiasts.

> ## *Serra da Estrela:*

The Serra da Estrela mountain range provides several options for trekking, skiing, and animal watching. Explore the lovely mountain communities of Manteigas and Covilhã, see the stunning landscape of the Torre, the highest point in mainland Portugal, and enjoy local delicacies like queijo da Serra, a wonderful sheep's milk cheese.

Tourists may make the most of their vacation to Northern Portugal by incorporating information about these local places, which will allow them to explore the region's various cultural, historical, and natural features.

HOW TO PLAN DAY TRIPS FROM MAJOR CITIES

Porto:

Day Trip to Douro Valley

Start your day early by visiting the Douro Valley, a UNESCO World Heritage Site noted for its magnificent vistas and world-renowned wine vineyards. Explore the lovely villages of Pinhão and Peso da Régua on a guided trip or by renting a car. Visit local vineyards for tastings and take a leisurely boat excursion down the Douro River.

Day Trip To Aveiro:

Explore the seaside city of Aveiro, sometimes known as the "Venice of Portugal," with its lovely canals and colorful Moliceiro boats. Spend the day touring the old city center, enjoying a boat trip around the canals, and sampling great local cuisine, such as ovos moles, a popular sweet delight.

Braga:

Day Trip to Guimarães:

Explore the ancient city of Guimarães, also known as the "birthplace of Portugal." Discover the UNESCO-listed Guimarães Castle, meander through the old town, and explore the Palace of the Dukes of Braganza. Don't pass up the opportunity to try local delicacies at one of the city's classic bars.

Day Trip To Bom Jesus do Monte:

Visit the famed Bom Jesus do Monte Sanctuary, which is located just outside of Braga. Take a picturesque trek or ride the funicular to the hilltop refuge, where you can appreciate the Baroque architecture and enjoy panoramic views of the surrounding environment.

Guimarães

Day Trip to Porto:
Take a quick train travel to Porto and spend the day visiting Portugal's second-largest city. Explore the ancient Ribeira neighborhood, including prominent monuments like the Dom Luís I Bridge and Livraria Lello bookshop. Sample port wine at one of the city's famed wine cellars along the waterfront.

Day Tour to Peneda-Gerês National Park:
Peneda-Gerês National Park, located near Guimarães, offers stunning natural beauty. Take a magnificent stroll through lush woods and steep terrain, see gorgeous towns, and cool down with a refreshing plunge in crystal-clear mountain streams.

When arranging day visits from Northern Portugal's major cities, consider transportation alternatives such as trains, buses, or rental vehicles, as well as journey time and attraction operating hours. Providing travelers with precise itineraries and logistical information will allow them to make the most of their day visits and create unforgettable experiences in Northern Portugal.

FAMILY-FRIENDLY ACTIVITIES

Attractions Suitable For Families With Children

➤ Porto Zoo (Zoólógico do Porto):

The Porto Zoo, located in the center of Porto, is an excellent family excursion. Lions, elephants, giraffes, and monkeys are among the animals that call the zoo their home. Visitors may experience guided tours, interactive animal encounters, and informative lectures. The zoo also has playgrounds, picnic spots, and food options, making it a great day out for the entire family.

➤ Sealife Porto:

Sea Life Porto is an immersive marine aquarium located near Matosinhos Beach. Families may explore intriguing underwater environments and get up close to aquatic species, including sharks, rays, seahorses, and octopuses. Children may learn about marine life and conservation firsthand through interactive displays, touch pools, and instructional seminars. Sea Life Porto also hosts unique events and activities throughout the year, making it an appealing location for families.

➤ Magicland Theme Park:

Magikland Theme Park, located in Penafiel, is Northern Portugal's largest amusement park, with a variety of rides, attractions, and entertainment for guests of every age. Families may experience thrilling roller coasters, water rides, carnival games, and live concerts and performances. Magikland has specific spaces for smaller children, like a kiddie carousel and a little train ride, so the whole family can have fun and excitement.

> ➢ *Pena Adventure Park:*

Pena Adventure Park, located in Ribeira de Pena, provides outdoor adventures and leisure activities in an environment rich in flora and natural sceneries. Families may engage in a range of activities, including zip line, treetop rope courses, and rock climbing. The park also has hiking paths, picnic spaces, and picturesque vistas, allowing families to interact with nature and enjoy outdoor activities together.

> ➢ *Portugal dos Pequenos*:

Portugal dos Pequenitos, or "Portugal for the Little Ones," is a delightful small park located in Coimbra. The park includes scaled-down versions of iconic Portuguese sights, such as castles, palaces, and traditional dwellings, which are intended to captivate the imagination of young visitors. Families may explore the small villages, gardens, and play areas, immersing themselves in Portuguese culture and history in an enjoyable and participatory manner.

Tourists visiting Northern Portugal with children may arrange unique and entertaining experiences by including information on these family-friendly activities, resulting in lasting memories for the entire family.

"I do believe it's time for another adventure"

CONCLUSION

As we near the end of our adventure across Northern Portugal, I hope you have been inspired and intrigued by the rich tapestry of experiences that this fascinating region has to offer. Northern Portugal offers a broad range of attractions, including the busy city streets of Porto, the calm landscapes of the Douro Valley, the ancient charm of Guimarães, and the spectacular beauty of the Peneda-Gerês National Park.

This book has covered the famous sites, cultural riches, and hidden jewels that distinguish Northern Portugal as a unique destination. We've learned about its rich history, enjoyed its delicious food, and immersed ourselves in its colorful culture. Whether you're a history buff, a foodie, a nature lover, or just looking for adventure, Northern Portugal has something for everyone.

But our adventure does not stop here. As you conclude this tour, I encourage you to take the next step and start on your own journey to Northern Portugal. Whether you're planning a family trip, a romantic break, or a single adventure, the beauties of Northern Portugal await you.

So pack your luggage today, and set your sights on adventure, and let the enchantment of Northern Portugal unfold in front of you. From the bustling streets of its towns to the quiet sands of its coastline, from the rolling hills of its countryside to the magnificent peaks of its mountains, Northern Portugal welcomes you to explore, discover, and have experiences that will last a lifetime.

Do not wait any longer. Begin arranging your trip to Northern Portugal today and discover the beauty, culture, and hospitality of this unique region for yourself. Your journey awaits

YOUR THOUGHTS

Dear Reader,

Thank you for choosing our travel guide to Northern Portugal as your companion on your journey through this captivating region. We hope that the insights, recommendations, and information provided within these pages have enriched your travel experience and inspired memorable adventures.

Your feedback is incredibly valuable to us. If you found our guide helpful, informative, and enjoyable, we would be immensely grateful if you could take a moment to leave a positive review. Your review will not only help other travelers discover the wonders of Northern Portugal but also provide us with valuable insights to improve future editions of our guide.

Your support enables us to continue creating high-quality travel resources and empowering travelers like yourself to explore the world with confidence and enthusiasm. So, please consider sharing your thoughts and experiences by leaving a review on your preferred platform.

Thank you for your support, and we look forward to hearing about your adventures in Northern Portugal!